A
BROADSIDE
TREASURY
1965–1970

A
BROADSIDE
TREASURY

1965-1970

Gwendolyn Brooks
Editor

bp

BROADSIDE PRESS

12651 Old Mill Place   Detroit, Michigan 48238

Acknowledgments

ALLEN, SAMUEL: from *Black Poetry*, 1969—View from the Corner. BRAD-
FORD, WALTER: T.C., Broadside No. 31. BROOKS, GWENDOLYN: from
Family Pictures—The Life of Lincoln West, Young Africans, Paul Robeson;
Martin Luther King, Jr. Memorial Broadside, 1968. DANNER, MARGARET:
from *Impressions of African Art Forms*, 1968—The Small Bells of Benin,
Etta Moten's Attic, The Convert. DAVIS, RONDA: Rip-Off, Broadside No.
40. EBON: from *Black Poetry*, 1969— To Our First Born. ECKELS, JON:
from *Home Is Where The Soul Is*, 1969—Hell, Mary. EMANUEL, JAMES:
from *The Treehouse*, 1968—The Negro, Freedom Rider: Washout, The Tree-
house, Fishermen; from *Panther Man*, 1970—Sixteen, Yeah, Whitey Baby.
FABIO, SARAH WEBSTER: Race Results, U.S.A., 1966—Broadside No. 14.
FOREMAN, KENT: from *For Malcolm*, 1967—Judgement Day. GIOVANNI,
NIKKI: from *Black Feeling Black Talk*, 1967—Poem (For BMC No. 1),
The True Import of Present Dialogue, Poem (No Name No. 3), Wilmington
Delaware, I'm Not Lonely, Black Power, Seduction; from *Black Judgement*,
1969—The Funeral of Martin Luther King, Knoxville Tennessee, Revolution-
ary Music, Beautiful Black Men, For Saundra, My Poem, Black Judgements;
from *Re:Creation*, 1970—Poem for Aretha, Alone, No Reservations, House-
cleaning, The Game of Game, Kidnap Poem, For A Lady of Pleasure Now
Retired, 2nd Rapp, A Robin's Poem, Toy Poem. HAMILTON, BOBB: A
Child's Nightmare, Broadside No. 9. HAYDEN, ROBERT: from *For Mal-
colm*—El-Hajj Malik El-Shabazz. HOAGLAND, EVERETT: from *Black
Velvet*, 1970—Prologue, Georgia—It's the Gospel Truth. JEFFERS, LANCE:
from *My Blackness Is The Beauty of This Land*, 1970—When She Spoke of
God, Vietnam: I Need More Than This Crust of Salt. JOANS, TED: from
For Malcolm, 1967—My Ace of Spades. JOHNSON, ALICIA L.: Our Days
Are Numbered, Broadside No. 30. JONES, LE ROI: from *For Malcolm*—
A Poem for Black Hearts. KGOSITSILE, KEORAPETSE W.: from *Spirits
Unchained*, 1969—When Brown Is Black, Mandela's Sermon, Elegy for
David Diop, Ivory Masks in Orbit, To Fanon; from *For Malcolm*, 1967—
Brother Malcolm's Echo. KILLEBREW, CARL: The Squared Circle, Broad-
side No. 29. KNIGHT, ETHERIDGE: from *Poems from Prison*, 1968—
Hard Rock, The Idea of Ancestry, As You Leave Me, The Violent Space,
2 Poems for Black Relocation Centers, It Was a Funky Deal, A Love Poem,
The Sun Came; from *Black Poetry*, 1969—For Black Poets Who Think of
Suicide. LEE, DON L.: from *Think Black*, 1967—Stereo, A Poem For Black
Women, In a Period of Growth, Awareness; from *Black Pride*, 1968—The
New Integrationist, The Cure All, Two Poems, Pains with a Light Touch,
The Self Hatred of Don L. Lee, In the Interest of Black Salvation, The Wall,
The Death Dance, The Traitor; from *Don't Cry, Scream*, 1969—But He Was
Cool, Don't Cry, Scream, Malcolm Spoke/Who Listened?, Assassination, A
Poem to Complement Other Poems, Blackmusic/a Beginning, BLACKWO-
MAN, The Revolutionary Screw, Reflections on a Lost Love, A Poem Look-
ing for a Reader, A Message All Blackpeople Can Dig; from *We Walk The
Way of The New World*, 1970—Mixed Sketches, On Seeing Diana Go
Madddddddd, A Poem for a Poet, Change Is Not Always Progress, For
Black People, Change-up, Move Un-noticed to be Noticed. LLORENS,
DAVID: from *For Malcolm*—One Year Ago. LONG, DOUGHTRY: from
Black Poetry—One Time Henry Dreamed the Number. MADGETT, NAOMI

5

LONG: Sunny, Broadside No. 11. MARVIN X: from *Black Man Listen*, 1969—Proverbs, Till the Sun Goes Down. NEAL, LAWRENCE P.: from *For Malcolm*—Malcolm X—An Autobiography, Morning Raga for Malcolm. PATTERSON, RAYMOND: from *For Malcolm*—At That Moment. PFISTER, ARTHUR: Granny Blak Poet (in Pastel), Broadside No. 35. RANDALL, DUDLEY: from *Cities Burning*, 1968—Roses and Revolutions, Primitives, The Rite, Hail Dionysos, Ballad of Birmingham; from *Black Poetry*, 1969—The Profile on the Pillow; from *Poem Counterpoem*, 1966— The Southern Road, George, Booker T. and W.E.B. RANDALL, JAMES: from *Don't Ask Me Who I Am*, 1970—Execution, Who Shall Die, My Childhood, Seascape. RAVEN, JOHN: from *Blues for Momma*, 1970—Assailant, The Roach, An Inconvenience. REESE, S. CAROLYN: Letter From a Wife, Broadside No. 12. RIVERS, CONRAD KENT: from *For Malcolm*—If Blood Is Black Then Spirit Neglects My Unborn Son. RODGERS, CAROLYN: Now Ain't That Love?, Broadside No. 37. RUTHERFORD, TONY (Umar Abd Rahim Hasson): Black and White, Broadside No. 28. SANCHEZ, SONIA: from *Homecoming*, 1969—To All Brothers, Poem at Thirty, Black Magic, Summary; from *We a BaddDDD People*, 1970—A Poem for My Father, A Needed Poem for My Salvation, We a BaddDDD People, Life Poem. So This Is Our Revolution, Let Us Begin the Real Work, A Ballad for Stirling Street; from *For Malcolm*—Malcolm. SPRIGGS, EDWARD: from *Black Poetry*—For the Truth; from *For Malcolm*—For Brother Malcolm. STEPHANY: from *Moving Deep*, 1969—Because I Have Wandered Long, My Love When This Is Past, Who Collects the Pain, You Are Instantly Enfolded. TOURE', ASKIA MUHAMMAD: Earth, Broadside No. 24. WALKER, MARGARET: from *Prophets for a New Day*, 1970—Prophets for a New Day, Jackson Mississippi, For Andy Goodman, Michael Schwerner, and James Chaney. WHITSITT, JOYCE: from *For Malcolm*—For Malcolm.

6

Contents

Introduction

Dudley Randall made a clean decision. He would create a Black platform. He would support and display the talents of vital Black poets who had besieged, overlong, the apathy of white publishers. He began by presenting, attractively, single poems on cards: broadsides. Slender paperbacks followed, then hard-covers. Then tapes, and records. Today, Broadside Press has a distinguished reputation as an assistant to the progress of most Black poet-stars of the day.

There have been changes in Black poetry since Don L. Lee, principal stimulus and influence of the "new breed," wrote that necessary Black poem "The New Integrationist":

> i
> seek
> integration
> of
> negroes
> with
> black
> people.

Many of the Broadside poets, through the language-testing years since 1966, have been achingly busy with maneuver and jolt, and the result is that, again and again, the astonished reader finds himself aware of an individual voice. He says "This poet sounds like *no one else.*" And this even though, early on, he has understood that *general* tools here are the hot hand, the hot heart, HARD health.

"There is a return to the folk," said Houston A. Baker in *Liberator.* Yes. And an agreeable invasion *of* the folk, an appropriation of supplies, wonderful supplies, *only* to shape, to fill, to enhance with substantial embroidery a fundamental strength, which is then *returned,* with proud respect.

This Treasury of Broadside publications is a provocative sampler of the recent contributing richness and Black dedication.

—*Gwendolyn Brooks*

13

From
For Malcolm

Ted Joans

MY ACE OF SPADES

MALCOLM X SPOKE TO ME and sounded you
Malcolm X said this to me & THEN TOLD you that!
Malcolm X whispered in my ears but SCREAMED
 on you!
Malcolm X praised me & condemned you
Malcolm X smiled at me & sneered at you
Malcolm X made me proud & so you got scared
Malcolm X told me to HURRY & you began to worry
Malcolm X sang to me but GROWLED AT YOU!!
Malcolm X words freed me & they frightened you
Malcolm X tol' it lak in DAMN SHO' IS!!
Malcolm X said that everybody will be F R E E ! !
Malcolm X said that everybody will be F R E E ! !
Malcolm X told both of us the T R U T H . . . . . .
                                    now didn't he?

Larry Neal

MALCOLM X—AN AUTOBIOGRAPHY

I am the Seventh Son of the Son
who was also the Seventh.
I have drunk deep of the waters of my ancestors
have traveled the soul's journey towards cosmic
          harmony
the Seventh son.
Have walked slick avenues
and seen grown men fall, to die in a blue doom
of death and ancestral agony,
have seen old men glide, shadowless, feet barely
touching the pavements.

I sprang out of the Midwestern plains
the bleak Michigan landscape wearing the slave name —
Malcolm Little.
Saw a brief vision in Lansing, when I was seven, and in

my mother's womb heard the beast cry of death,
a landscape on which white robed figures ride, and my
Garvey father silhouetted against the night-fire, gun
        in hand
form outlined against a panorama of violence.

Out of the midwestern bleakness, I sprang, pushed
        eastward,
past shack on country nigger shack, across the
        wilderness
of North America.
I hustler. I pimp. I unfulfilled black man
bursting with destiny.
New York city Slim called me Big Red,
and there was no escape, close nights of the smell
        of death.
Pimp. Hustler. The day fills these rooms.

I am talking about New York. Harlem.
talking about the neon madness.
talking about ghetto eyes and nights
about death oozing across the room. Small's paradise.
talking about cigarette butts, and rooms smelly
        with white
sex flesh, and dank sheets, and being on the run.
talking about cocaine illusions, about stealing
        and selling.
talking about these New York cops who smell of
        blood and money.
I am Big Red, tiger vicious, Big Red, bad nigger, will kill.

But there is rhythm here. Its own special substance:
I hear Billie sing, no good man, and dig Prez, wearing
        the Zoot
suit of life, the pork-pie hat tilted at the correct angle.
through the Harlem smoke of beer and whiskey, I
        understand the
mystery of the signifying monkey,
in a blue haze of inspiration, I reach for the totality
        of Being.
I am at the center of a swirl of events. War and death.
rhythm. hot women. I think life a commodity
        bargained for

across the bar in Small's.
I perceive the echoes of Bird and there is gnawing in
        the maw
of my emotions.
and then there is jail. America is the world's
        greatest jailer,
and we all in jails. Black spirits contained like
        magnificent
birds of wonder. I now understand my father urged
        on by the ghost of Garvey
and see a small black man standing in a corner. The
        cell, cold.
dank. The light around him vibrates. Am I crazy? But
        to under-
stand is to submit to a more perfect will, a more perfect
        order,
to understand is to surrender the imperfect self,
for a more perfect self.

Allah formed black man, I follow
and shake within the very depth of my most imperfect
        being,
and I bear witness to the Message of Allah
and I bear witness—all praise is due Allah!

MORNING RAGA FOR MALCOLM

I
O Allah . . . receive him, a morning god
bursting springly in ascendant
colors of the sun—a crescent sword slices
the shrill morning raga; in the place
of his hajih the voice tears at blood
streaked faces. dispossessed eyes flash at
the truth brilliantly black.
a gnawing, pounding skin ripping voice
that does not back down—O Allah, great Spirit One
receive the gritting teeth, the bursting balls,
mangled bodies, ripped out guts spewed from piss pot
to armchair deaths. . . .

receive the unfulfilled, the unavenged; these hordes.
one expanded nigger face explodes in time, screaming
ghostly scorching everything in sight—Great Spirit One

II
I awake to see my ears and arms flying into space
to feel my legs violently crack as I stretch
for another planet: blue free voice. see free voices
    spin bluely.
spin bluely spin. spin blood hopes spin. spin resurrected
    god.

I now calm airly float
lift my spirit—Allah you
am me. space undulates.
under me, space, to my sides
and under me nothing
I now calm airly float.

Robert Hayden

EL-HAJJ MALIK EL-SHABAZZ

(Malcolm X)

> *O masks and metamorphoses of Ahab,*
> *Native Son*

I.
The icy evil that struck his father down
and ravished his mother into madness
trapped him in violence of a punished self
raging to break free.

As Home Boy, as Dee-troit Red,
he fled his name, became the quarry of
his own obsessed pursuit.

He conked his hair and Lindy-hopped,
zoot-suited jiver, swinging those chicks
in the hot rose and reefer glow.

His injured childhood bullied him.
He skirmished in the Upas trees
and cannibal flowers of the American Dream—

But could not hurt the enemy
powered against him there.

II.
Sometimes the dark that gave his life
its cold satanic sheen would shift
a little, and he saw himself
floodlit and eloquent;

Yet how could he, "Satan" in The Hole,
guess what the waking dream prefigured?

Then black light of partial vision came:
He fell upon his face before
a racist Allah pledged to wrest him from
the hellward-dipping hands of Calvin's Christ—

To free him and his kind
from Yakub's white-faced treachery.
He rose redeemed from all but prideful anger,

Though adulterate attars could
not cleanse him of the odors of the pit.

III.
Asalam alaikum!

He X'd his name, became his people's anger,
exhorted them to vengeance for their past;
rebuked, admonished them,

Their scourger who
would shame them, drive them
from the lush ice gardens of their servitude.

Asalam alaikum!

Rejecting Ahab, he was of Ahab's tribe.
"Strike through the mask!"

IV.
Time. "The martyr's time," he said.
Time and the karate killer,
knifer, gunman. Time that brought
ironic trophies as his faith

Twined sparking round the bole,
the fruit of neo-Islam.
"The martyr's time."

But first, the ebb time pilgrimage
toward revelation, Hejira to
his final metamorphosis:

Labbayk! Labbayk!

He fell upon his face before
Allah the raceless in whose blazing Oneness all

Were one. He rose renewed, renamed, became
much more than there was time for him to be.

David Llorens

ONE YEAR AGO

Again he strode forward
And they waited
Escaping the grapes
The needle
The lies
For moments of hope
They knew
His heart filled with song
But he was not a
Singer

But more a choir
Of Truth
And some unfriendly
Victimized
Arose
Noise! Destruction! Hell!
But even while
Crying
They were glad
He didn't
Die
Big Red

Joyce Whitsitt Lawrence
(Malaika Wangara)

FOR MALCOLM

Oh beautiful, black martyr
Cut down by guns held in black hands,
You and they, proclaiming the worth of being black,
But they, somehow deaf to tones of truth
Issuing from your golden black throat,
Feared for their song of hate
And in jealousy borne for your mingled melodies
    Of brotherhood, black brotherhood
    And strength, violent if need be
    With pride of real negritude,
Cut you down.

Were you to be the leader
Of a new flock from the dark skinned nation,
The mastermind of precisioned flight
Long grounded by fledglings
Grovelling in shadows of white fathers?

You were the brilliant embodiment
Of elusive manhood. Those who are less
Negate your death and fail to acknowledge
Righteousness felt of your logic.

Oh beautiful, black martyr
Cut down by black hands,
Held down by little white minds,
Send back your song to a century wrong
Yet seeking one of your golden throat
Your growing notes of truth.

Conrad Kent Rivers

IF BLOOD IS BLACK THEN SPIRIT
NEGLECTS MY UNBORN SON

For Malcolm X in Substance

You must remember structures beyond cotton plains
        filled
            by joes voting for godot,
                stealing the white man's thunder,
                    avarice,

                Songs of silence parade your dead body
                Distracted by housemaids' bending backs
                Gold dusted, not sinned in the angry silence
                Surrounding fetid breaths and heavy sighs
                As your actor friend tells of tall trees
                Addressing that tenth talented mind
                Bowing for recognition under the sun shining
                Cameras shaping your body

You must remember that and this second whirl of
        care
            while black brothers grieve
                your unbroken Upanishads passing the white
                    man's understanding of your new peace
            without hate.
                Your new love with sweet words
            articulating complete manhood,
                directly questioning the whole and famous
            words you said.
                Let my women mourn for days
        in flight.

Sonia Sanchez

MALCOLM

Do not speak to me of martyrdom
of men who die to be remembered
on some parish day.
I don't believe in dying
though I too shall die
and violets like castanets
will echo me.

Yet this man
this dreamer,
thick-lipped with words
will never speak again
and in each winter
when the cold air cracks
with frost, I'll breathe
his breath and mourn
my gun-filled nights.

He was the sun that tagged
the western sky and
melted tiger-scholars
while they searched for stripes.
He said, "Fuck you white
man. we have been
curled too long. nothing
is sacred now. not your
white face nor any
land that separates
until some voices
squat with spasms."

Do not speak to me of living.
life is obscene with crowds
of white on black.
death is my pulse.
what might have been
is not for him/or me
but what could have been
floods the womb until I drown.

Kent Foreman

JUDGEMENT DAY: FOR BIG RED
THE DARWINIAN DOGE.
R.I.P.

Yesterday was Doomsday.
. . . . Ask Miles—
Yesterday was Doomsday.
And Mutants will Arise,
Have risen.
They infiltrate the walls of prison
Wombs . . . .
Doomsday was yesterday . . . .

Today
Fred Nietszche's tarbrush children,
FAST!
Sit gassed
In Hyde Park cellars
Speaking in frown-invoking idioms
Of swirling spiral nebuli
And Aunt Samantha's sweet potato pie
And Sartre
On many levels
Devils they were
Yesterday
Was Doomsday . . . .

So Androids
Mesmerized by T.V. sets
Or biblical cartoons
Avoid
Wistful regrets
As grey baboons
Housebroken pets . . . .

Was yesterday really Doomsday?

So Zombies
Garbed by
Abercrombie & Fitch
Not swift enough to scratch their

Itching souls
        Like moles
            In a frenzy
        Burrow holes
            In quicksand . . . .

Yesterday was Doomsday
                    But
        Why scare
        The unaware
            I doubt if the Neanderthaler feared
            The hour when Cro-Magnon mind appeared.

The Oracles in tombs say:
"Yesterday was Doomsday . . . ."

Keorapetse W. Kgositsile

BROTHER MALCOLM'S ECHO

                Translated furies ring
                on the page not thoughts
                about life
                but what should be
                real people and things
                loving love
                this is real
                the human Spirit moves
                what should be
                grinning molotov cocktails
                replenishing the fire
                WATTS happening
                SHARPEVILLE burning
                much too damn talking
                is not
                what's happening

LeRoi Jones
(Imamu Amiri Baraka)

A POEM FOR BLACK HEARTS

For Malcolm's eyes, when they broke
the face of some dumb white man. For
Malcolm's hands raised to bless us
all black and strong in his image
of ourselves, for Malcolm's words
fire darts, the victor's tireless
thrusts, words hung above the world
change as it may, he said it, and
for this he was killed, for saying,
and feeling, and being/change, all
collected hot in his heart, For Malcolm's
heart, raising us above our filthy cities,
for his stride, and his beat, and his address
to the grey monsters of the world, For Malcolm's
pleas for your dignity, black men, for your life,
black men, for the filling of your minds
with righteousness, For all of him dead and
gone and vanished from us, and all of him which
clings to our speech black god of our time.
For all of him, and all of yourself, look up,
black man, quit stuttering and shuffling, look up,
black man, quit whining and stooping, for all of him,
For Great Malcolm a prince of the earth, let nothing
    in us rest
until we avenge ourselves for his death, stupid animals
that killed him, let us never breathe a pure breath if
we fail, and white men call us faggots till the end of
the earth.

Raymond Patterson

AT THAT MOMENT

When they shot Malcolm Little down
On the stage of the Audubon Ballroom,
When his life ran out through bullet holes
(Like the people running out when the murder began)
His blood soaked the floor
One drop found a crack through the stark
Pounding thunder—slipped under the stage and began
Its journey: burrowed through concrete into the cellar,
Dropped down darkness exploding like quicksilver
Pellets of light, panicking rats, paralyzing cockroaches—
Tunneled through rubble and wrecks of foundations,
The rocks that buttress the bowels of the city, flowed
Into pipes and powerlines, the mains and cables of
    the city:
A thousand fiery seeds.

At that moment,
Those who drank water where he entered . . .
Those who cooked food where he passed . . .
Those who burned light while he listened . . .
Those who were talking as he went, knew he was water
Running out of faucets, gas running out of jets, power
Running out of sockets, meaning running along taut
    wires—
To the hungers of their living. It was said
Whole slums of clotted Harlem plumbing groaned
And sundered free that day, and disconnected gas
    and light
Went on and on and on . . .
They rushed his riddled body on a stretcher
To the hospital. But the police were too late.
It had already happened.

Edward S. Spriggs

FOR BROTHER MALCOLM

there is no memorial site
in harlem
save the one we are building
in the street of
our young minds
till our hands & eyes
have strength to mould
the concrete beneath our feet

Poets

Gwendolyn Brooks

THE LIFE OF LINCOLN WEST

Ugliest little boy
that everyone ever saw.
That is what everyone said.

Even to his mother it was apparent—
when the blue-aproned nurse came into the
northeast end of the maternity ward
bearing his squeals and plump bottom
looped up in a scant receiving blanket,
bending, to pass the bundle carefully
into the waiting mother-hands—that this
was no cute little ugliness, no sly baby waywardness
that was going to inch away
as would baby fat, baby curl, and
baby spot-rash. The pendulous lip, the
branching ears, the eyes so wide and wild,
the vague unvibrant brown of the skin,
and, most disturbing, the great head.
These components of That Look bespoke
the sure fibre. The deep grain.

His father could not bear the sight of him.
His mother high-piled her pretty dyed hair and
put him among her hairpins and sweethearts,
dance slippers, torn paper roses.
He was not less than these,
he was not more.

As the little Lincoln grew,
uglily upward and out, he began
to understand that something was
wrong. His little ways of trying
to please his father, the bringing
of matches, the jumping aside at
warning sound of oh-so-large and
rushing stride, the smile that gave
and gave and gave—Unsuccessful!

Even Christmases and Easters were spoiled.
He would be sitting at the
family feasting table, really
delighting in the displays of mashed potatoes
and the rich golden
fat-crust of the ham or the festive
fowl, when he would look up and find
somebody feeling indignant about him.

What a pity what a pity. No love
for one so loving. The little Lincoln
loved Everybody. Ants. The changing
caterpillar. His much-missing mother.
His kindergarten teacher.

His kindergarten teacher—whose
concern for him was composed of one
part sympathy and two parts repulsion.
The others ran up with their little drawings.
He ran up with his.
She
tried to be as pleasant with him as
with others, but it was difficult.
For she was all pretty! all daintiness,
all tiny vanilla, with blue eyes and fluffy
sun-hair. One afternoon she
saw him in the hall looking bleak against
the wall. It was strange because the
bell had long since rung and no other
child was in sight. Pity flooded her.
She buttoned her gloves and suggested
cheerfully that she walk him home. She
started out bravely, holding him by the
hand. But she had not walked far before
she regretted it. The little monkey.
Must everyone look? And clutching her
hand like that . . . Literally pinching
it . . .

At seven, the little Lincoln loved
the brother and sister who
moved next door. Handsome. Well-

dressed. Charitable, often, to him. They
enjoyed him because he was
resourceful, made up
games, told stories. But when
their More Acceptable friends came they turned
their handsome backs on him. He
hated himself for his feeling
of well-being when with them despite—
Everything.

He spent much time looking at himself
in mirrors. What could be done?
But there was no
shrinking his head. There was no
binding his ears.

"Don't touch me!" cried the little
fairy-like being in the playground.

Her name was Nerissa. The many
children were playing tag, but when
he caught her, she recoiled, jerked free
and ran. It was like all the
rainbow that ever was, going off
forever, all, all the sparklings in
the sunset west.

One day, while he was yet seven,
a thing happened. In the down-town movies
with his mother a white
man in the seat beside him whispered
loudly to a companion, and pointed at
the little Linc.
"THERE! That's the kind I've been wanting
to show you! One of the best
examples of the specie. Not like
those diluted Negroes you see so much of on
the streets these days, but the
real thing.

Black, ugly, and odd. You
can see the savagery. The blunt

blankness. That is the real
thing."

His mother—her hair had never looked so
red around the dark brown
velvet of her face—jumped up,
shrieked "Go to —" She did not finish.
She yanked to his feet the little
Lincoln, who was sitting there
staring in fascination at his assessor. At the author of his
new idea.

All the way home he was happy. Of course,
he had not liked the word
"ugly."
But, after all, should he not
be used to that by now? What had
struck him, among words and meanings
he could little understand, was the phrase
"the real thing."
He didn't know quite why,
but he liked that.
He liked that very much.

When he was hurt, too much
stared at—
too much
left alone—he
thought about that. He told himself
"After all, I'm
the real thing."

It comforted him.

YOUNG AFRICANS

of the furious

Who take Today and jerk it out of joint
have made new underpinnings and a Head.

Blacktime is time for chimeful
poemhood
but they decree a
jagged chiming now.

If there are flowers flowers
must come out to the road. Rowdy!—
knowing where wheels and people are,
knowing where whips and screams are,
knowing where deaths are, where the kind kills are.

As for that other kind of kindness,
if there is milk it must be mindful.
The milkofhumankindness must be mindful
as wily wines.
Must be fine fury.
Must be mega, must be main.

Taking Today (to jerk it out of joint)
the hardheroic maim the
leechlike-as-usual who use,
adhere to, carp, and harm.

And they await,
across the Changes and the spiraling dead,
our black revival, our black vinegar,
our hands, and our hot blood.

PAUL ROBESON

That time
we all heard it,
cool and clear,
cutting across the hot grit of the day.
The major Voice.
The adult Voice
forgoing Rolling River,
forgoing tearful tale of bale and barge
and other symptoms of an old despond.
Warning, in music-words
devout and large,
that we are each other's
harvest:
we are each other's
business:
we are each other's
magnitude and bond.

Margaret Danner

THE SMALL BELLS OF BENIN

Here in a Chicago museum, these small bells of
    Benin,
without ringing, are bringing their charm to a
    foreign scene.

The concave cylindrical draping of some
is as prim as the pose of a Quaker maid.
While the rare quadrangular forms of the rest
with their molded latticed designs, suggest
the iron fences displayed

in New Orleans, and who can escape
the quaint, spellbound, gargoyle-like
bronze faces that stare from their settings
of thin metal lace?

I wish I could obtain one of these bells
or even a facsimile, but the formula
to their deft mouldings was lost
and hasn't been quite reproduced or found.

ETTA MOTEN'S ATTIC

It was as if Gaugin
had upset a huge paintpot
of his incomparable tangerine,

splashing wherever my startled eyes ran
here, there and at my very hand on
masks and carvings and paintings not seen

here before; spilling straight as a stripe
spun geometrically in Ndebele rug
flung over an ebony chair,

or dripping round as a band on a type
of bun the Watusi warriors
make of their pompadoured hair,

39

splashing high as a sunbird or fly moving
over a frieze of mahogany trees,
or splotching out from low underneath as a root,

shimmering bright as a ladybug, grooving
a green bed of moss, sparkling as a beetle,
a bee, shockingly dotting the snoot

of an ape or the nape of its neck or as clue
to its navel, stamping a Zulu's
intriguing mask, tipping

the lips of a chief of Ashanti's who
was carved to his stool so he'd sit
there forever and never fear a slipping

of rule or command, dyeing the skirt
(all askew) that wouldn't stay put on the
Pygmy in spite of his real leather belt,

quickening and charming till we felt the bloom
of veldt and jungle flow through the room.

THE CONVERT

When in nineteen-thirty-seven, Etta Moten, sweet-
    heart
of our Art Study group, kept her promise, as if
    clocked,
to honor my house at our first annual tea, my
    pride

tipped the sky, but when she, Parisian-poised and I
    as smart
as a chrome-toned page from Harper's Bazaar, gave
    my shocked
guests this hideous African nude, I could have
    cried.

And for many subsequent suns, we, who had placed
    apart

this hour to drum for our plunge into modern art,
    mocked
her. "Isn't he lovely?" whenever we eyed this
    thing,

for by every rule we'd learned, we'd been led to
    discern
this rankling figure as ugly. It hunched in a
    squat
as if someone with maliciously disfiguring intent

had flattened it with a press, bashing its head,
bloating its features, making huge bulging blots
of its lips and nose, and as my eyes in dread
    anticipation

pulled downward, there was its navel, without a
    thread
of covering, ruptured, exposed, protruding from
    a pot
stomach as huge as a mother's-to-be, on short,
    bent legs,

extending as far on each side as swollen back limbs
of a turtle. I could look no farther and nearly
    dispensed
with being polite while pretending to welcome her
    gift.

But afterwards, to the turn of calendar pages, my
    eyes would skim
the figure, appraising this fantastic sight,
until, finally, I saw on its

ebony face, not a furniture polished, shellacked
    shine,
but a radiance, gleaming as though a small light
had flashed internally: and I could discern

through the sheen that the bulging eyes
were identical twins to the bulging nose.
The same symmetrical form was dispersed again

and again through all the bulges; the thighs

and the hands and lips, in reverse, even the toes
of this fast turning beautiful form were a self-
    same chain,

matching the navel. This little figure stretched
    high
in grace, in its with-the-grain form and from-
    within-glow,
in its curves in concord. I became a hurricane

of elation, a convert undaunted, who wanted to
    flaunt
her discovery, flourish her fair-figured find.

Art clubs like leaves in autumn, fall,
scrabble against concrete and scatter.
And Etta Moten, I read, is at tea with the Queen.

But I find myself still framing word sketches
of how much these blazing forms ascending the
    centuries
in their muted sheens, matter to me.

Jon Eckels

HELL, MARY

Hell, Mary
Bell Jones,
full of groans
the slum lord
is on you
Cursed are you
among women
and cursed is
the fruit of
your womb,
Willie Lee,
as it was
in 1619
is now
and ever
shall be
SHIT
without end
            Amen

James Emanuel

THE NEGRO

Never saw him.
Never can.
Hypothetical,
Haunting man:

Eyes a-saucer,
Yessir bossir,
Dice a-clicking,
Razor flicking.

The-ness froze him
In a dance.
A-ness never
Had a chance.

FREEDOM RIDER: WASHOUT

The first blow hurt.
(God is love, is love.)
My blood spit into the dirt.
(Sustain my love, oh, Lord above!)
Curses circled one another.
(They were angry with their brother.)

I was too weak
For this holy game.
A single freckled fist
Knocked out the memory of His name.
Bloody, I heard a long, black moan,
Like waves from slave ships long ago.
With Gabriel Prosser's dogged knuckles
I struck an ancient blow.

THE TREEHOUSE

To every man
His treehouse,
A green splice in the humping years,
Spartan with narrow cot
And prickly door.

To every man
His twilight flash
Of luminous recall
 of tiptoe years
 in leaf-stung flight;
 of days of squirm and bite
 that waved antennas through the grass;
 of nights
 when every moving thing
 was girlshaped,
 expectantly turning.

To every man
His house below
And his house above—
With perilous stairs
Between.

FISHERMEN

When three, he fished these lakes,
Curled sleeping on a lip of rock,
Crib blankets tucked from ants and fishbone flies,
Twitching as the strike of bass and snarling reel
Uncoiled my shouts not quit
Till he jerked blinking up on all-fours,
Swaying with the winking leaves.
Strong awake, he shook his cane pole like a spoon
And dipped among the wagging perch
Till, tired, he drew his silver rubber blade
And poked the winding fins that tugged our string,
Or sprayed the dimpling minnows with his plastic gun,
Or, rainstruck, squirmed to my armpit in the poncho.

45

Ten years uncurled him, thinned him hard.
Now, far he casts his line into the wrinkled blue
And easy toes a rock, reel on his thigh
Till bone and crank cry out the strike
He takes with manchild chuckles, cunning
In his play of zigzag line and plunging silver.

Now fishing far from me, he strides through rain, shoulders
A spiny ridge of pines, and disappears
Near lakes that cannot be, while I must choose
To go or stay: bring blanket, blade, and gun,
Or stand a fisherman.

SIXTEEN, YEAH

Practices brutality closing doors
twisting screams from stereo
when company brings a girl
whose eyes take chances;
papers his bedside wall with aluminum foil
that shivercrackles lively breeze
can't slow its dance with shoebox
rigged with Christmas bulbs
that flash whole cities through the air;
sleeps in his schoolclothes
lulled in pockets of his mind
untouched unlit
except by underside of things beyond
like movies plays and skirts
somebody names then winks his eye.

Knows the wink is all
feels the door the scream the silly foil
that dances in the dark
naked in the skirt.

Practices brutality
sleeps with his fingers
in some other hand
and can't lie still
near music.

WHITEY, BABY

WhatCHU care
what I feel
when I think blk
pull down the shades / on my mind
turn my back t yr hand
putcha outa my room
digya outa my life?

WhatCHU know
bout stayin in the dark
cause ya cant blieve nothin
nobody says / bout good things
ya gonna get
xcep somethin Mama made?

WhatCHU know
bout Daddy comin home fired
cause crackers tricked m
out s job,
and broodin in s broken chair
takin a hour takin off s coat?

Gonna show / you / KNOW
by shakin yr hair
sadlike, wearin tighter pants
on trips,
puttin a button where yr heart is.

Who ya gonna TELL, baby,
when ya feel / I dont care
anymore?

What THEY care
whatchu feel?

Nikki Giovanni

POEM (For BMC No. 1)

I stood still and was a mushroom on the forest green
With all the moiles conferring as to my edibility
It stormed and there was no leaf to cover me
I was water-logged (having absorbed all that I could)
I dreamed I was drowning
That no sun from Venice would dry my tears
But a silly green cricket with a pink umbrella said
Hello Tell me about it
And we talked our way through the storm

Perhaps we could have found an Inn
Or at least a rainbow somewhere over
But they always said
Only one Only one more
And Christmas being so near
We over identified

Though I worship nothing (save myself)
You were my savior—so be it
And it was
Perhaps not never more or ever after
But after all—once you were mine

6-'67

THE TRUE IMPORT OF PRESENT DIALOGUE BLACK VS. NEGRO

(For Peppi, Who Will Ultimately Judge Our Efforts)

Nigger
Can you kill
Can you kill
Can a nigger kill
Can a nigger kill a honkie
Can a nigger kill the Man
Can you kill nigger
Huh? nigger can you
kill

48

Do you know how to draw blood
Can you poison
Can you stab-a-jew
Can you kill huh? nigger
Can you kill
Can you run a protestant down with your
'68 El Dorado
(that's all they're good for anyway)
Can you kill
Can you piss on a blond head
Can you cut it off
Can you kill
A nigger can die
We ain't got to prove we can die
We got to prove we can kill
They sent us to kill
Japan and Africa
We policed europe
Can you kill
Can you kill a white man
Can you kill the nigger
in you
Can you make your nigger mind
die
Can you kill your nigger mind
And free your black hands to
strangle
Can you kill
Can a nigger kill
Can you shoot straight and
Fire for good measure
Can you splatter their brains in the street
Can you kill them
Can you lure them to bed to kill them
We kill in Viet Nam
for them
We kill for UN & NATO & SEATO & US
and everywhere for all alphabet but
BLACK
Can we learn to kill WHITE for BLACK
Learn to kill niggers
Learn to be Black men

1-'68

49

POEM (No Name No. 3)

The Black Revolution is passing you bye
negroes
Anne Frank didn't put cheese and bread away for you
Because she knew it would be different this time
The naziboots don't march this year
Won't march next year
Won't come to pick you up in a
honka honka VW bus
So, don't wait for that
negroes
They already got Malcolm
They already got LeRoi
They already strapped a harness on Rap
They already pulled Stokely's teeth
They already here if you can hear properly
negroes
Didn't you hear them when 10 thousand indians died from
    exposure to
honkies
Didn't you hear them when viet children died from exposure to
napalm
Can't you hear them when arab women die from exposure to
isrealijews
You hear them while you die from exposure to wine and poverty
    programs
If you hear properly
negroes
Tomorrow was too late to properly arm yourself
See can you do an improper job now
See can you do now something, anything, but move now
negro
If the Black Revolution passes you by it's for damned sure
the whi-te reaction to it won't

1-'68

50

WILMINGTON DELAWARE

Wilmington is a funni negro
He's a cute little gingerbread man who stuffs his pipe with
Smog and gas fumes and maybe (if you promise not to tale)
just a little bit of . . . pot
Because he has to meet his maker each and everyday
LORD KNOWS HE'S A GOOD BOY AND TRIES HARD
While most of us have to go to church only once a week

They tell me he's up for the coloredman of the year award
And he'll probably win
(If he'd just stop wetting on himself each and everytime he
meets a Due-pontee)
LORD KNOWS HE TRIES

Why just the other day I heard him say NO
But he was only talking to the janitor and I believe they
expect him to exercise some control over the excretionary
facilities around here
(But it's a start)

My only real criticism is that he eats his daily nourishment at the
    "Y"
And I was taught that's not proper to do in public

But he's sharp, my but that boy is sharp
Why it took the overlords two generations to recognize that negroes
had moved to the East side of town (which is similar to but not the
same as the wrong side of the tracks)
And here he is making plans for future whites who haven't even
reclaimed the best land yet

"Don't say nothing Black or colored or look unhappy"
I heard him tell his chief joints . . .
And every bone bopped in place but quick
(He can really order some colored people around . . . a sight
to behold)
And does a basically good militant shuffle when dancing is in
order

I'd really like to see him party more but he swears
Asphalt is bad for his eye-talian shoes

And we all appreciate eye-tal
don't we

I tried to talk to him once but he just told me
"Don't be emotional"
And all the while he was shaking and crying and raining blows
on poor black me

So I guess I'm wrong again
Just maybe I don't know the colour of my
truefriends
As Wilmington pointed out to me himself

But I'm still not going to anymore banquits

The last one they replaced jello with
jellied gas (a Due-pontee speciality; housewise)
And I couldn't figure out what they were trying to tell me
Wilmington said they were giving me guest treat-meants

But some how I don't feel welcome
So I'm going to pack my don-key (ass wise) and split
before they start to do me favors too

1-'67

I'M NOT LONELY

i'm not lonely
sleeping all alone

you think i'm scared
but i'm a big girl
i don't cry
or anything

i have a great
big bed
to roll around
in and lots of space
and i don't dream
bad dreams
like i used
to have that you

were leaving me
anymore

now that you're gone
i don't dream
and no matter
what you think
i'm not lonely
sleeping
all alone

12-'68

BLACK POWER

(For All The Beautiful Black Panthers East)

But the whole thing is a miracle—See?

We were just standing there
Talking—not touching or smoking
Pot
When this cop told
Tyrone
Move along buddy—take your whores
Outa here

And this tremendous growl
From out of nowhere
Pounced on him

Nobody to this very day
Can explain
How it happened

And none of the zoos or circuses
Within fifty miles
Had reported
A panther
Missing.

5-'66

SEDUCTION

one day
you gonna walk in this house
and i'm gonna have on a long African
gown
you'll sit down and say "The Black . . ."
and i'm gonna take one arm out
then you—not noticing me at all— will say "What about
    this brother . . ."
and i'm going to be slipping it over my head
and you'll rap on about "The Revolution . . ."
while i rest your hand against my stomach
you'll go on—as you always do—saying "I just can't dig . . ."
while i'm moving your hand up and down
and i'll be taking your dashiki off
then you'll say "What we really need . . ."
and i'll be licking your arm
and "The way I see it we ought to . . ."
and unbuckling your pants
"And what about the situation . . ."
and taking your shorts off
then you'll notice
your state of undress
and knowing you you'll just say
"Nikki,
isn't this counterrevolutionary . . .?"

                                        12-17-'68

THE FUNERAL OF MARTIN LUTHER KING, JR.

His headstone said
FREE AT LAST, FREE AT LAST
But death is a slave's freedom
We seek the freedom of free men
And the construction of a world
Where Martin Luther King could have lived and preached non-violence

                                        Atlanta
                                        4-9-'68

54

KNOXVILLE, TENNESSEE

I always like summer
best
you can eat fresh corn
from daddy's garden
and okra
and greens
and cabbage
and lots of
barbecue
and buttermilk
and homemade ice-cream
at the church picnic
and listen to
gospel music
outside
at the church
homecoming
and go to the mountains with
your grandmother
and go barefooted
and be warm
all the time
not only when you go to bed
and sleep
                5-17-'68

REVOLUTIONARY MUSIC

you've just got to dig sly
and the family stone
damn the words
you gonna be dancing to the music
james brown can go to
viet nam
or sing about whatever he
has to
since he already told
the honkie
"although you happy you better try

55

to get along
money won't change you
but time is taking you on"
not to mention
doing a whole
song they can't even snap
their fingers to
"good god! ugh!"
talking bout
"i got the feeling baby i got the feeling"
and "hey everybody let me tell you the news"
martha and the vandellas dancing in the streets
while shorty long is functioning at that junction
yeah we hip to that
aretha said they better
think
but she already said
"ain't no way to love you"
(and you know she wasn't talking to us)
and dig the o'jays asking "must i always be a stand in
for love"
i mean they say "i'm a fool for being myself"

While the mighty mighty impressions have told the world
for once and for all
"We're a Winner"
even our names—le roi has said—are together
impressions
supremes
delfonics
miracles
intruders (i mean intruders?)
not beatles and animals and white bad things like
young rascals and shit
we be digging all
our revolutionary music consciously or un
cause sam cooke said "a change is gonna come"
                                                    7-'68

BEAUTIFUL BLACK MEN   (with compliments and apologies to all not mentioned by name)

i wanta say just gotta say something
bout those beautiful beautiful beautiful outasight
black men
with they afros
walking down the street
is the same ol danger
but a brand new pleasure

sitting on stoops, in bars, going to offices
running numbers, watching for their whores
preaching in churches, driving their hogs
walking their dogs, winking at me
in their fire red, lime green, burnt orange
royal blue tight tight pants that hug
what i like to hug

jerry butler, wilson pickett, the impressions
temptations, mighty mighty sly
don't have to do anything but walk
on stage
and i scream and stamp and shout
see new breed men in breed alls
dashiki suits with shirts that match
the lining that compliments the ties
that smile at the sandals
where dirty toes peek at me
and i scream and stamp and shout
for more beautiful beautiful beautiful
black men with outasight afros

9-10-'68

FOR SAUNDRA

i wanted to write
a poem
that rhymes
but revolution doesn't lend
itself to be-bopping

then my neighbor
who thinks i hate
asked—do you ever write
tree poems—i like trees
so i thought
i'll write a beautiful green tree poem
peeked from my window
to check the image
noticed the school yard was covered
with asphalt
no green—no trees grow
in manhattan

then, well, i thought the sky
i'll do a big blue sky poem
but all the clouds have winged
low since no-Dick was elected

so i thought again
and it occurred to me
maybe i shouldn't write
at all
but clean my gun
and check my kerosene supply

perhaps these are not poetic
times
at all

8-'68

MY POEM

i am 25 years old
black female poet
wrote a poem asking
nigger can you kill
if they kill me
it won't stop
the revolution

i have been robbed
it looked like they knew
that i was to be hit

they took my tv
my two rings
my piece of african print
and my two guns
if they take my life
it won't stop
the revolution

my phone is tapped
my mail is opened
they've caused me to turn
on all my old friends
and all my new lovers
if i hate all black
people
and all negroes
it won't stop
the revolution

i'm afraid to tell
my roommate where i'm going
and scared to tell
people if i'm coming
if i sit here
for the rest
of my life
it won't stop
the revolution

if i never write
another poem
or short story
if i flunk out
of grad school
if my car is reclaimed
and my record player
won't play
and if i never see
a peaceful day
or do a meaningful
black thing
it won't stop
the revolution

the revolution
is in the streets
and if i stay on
the 5th floor
it will go on
if i never do
anything
it will go on

10-3-'68

BLACK JUDGEMENTS
(of bullshit niggerish ways)

You
with your bullshit niggerish ways
want to destroy me

You want to preach
responsible revolution
along with progressive
procreation

Your desires will not be honored
this season

Shivering under the armour
of your
white protector
fear not
for thou art evil

The audacity of wanting
to be near the life
of what you seek to kill

Can you love
can you hate
is your game any damn good

Black Judgements are upon you
Black Judgements are upon you

4-'68

60

HOUSECLEANING

i always liked house cleaning
even as a child
i dug straightening
the cabinets
putting new paper on
the shelves
washing the refrigerator
inside out
and unfortunately this habit has
carried over and i find
i must remove you
from my life
                    1-11-'70

POEM FOR ARETHA

cause nobody deals with aretha—a mother with four
    children—having to hit the road
they always say "after she comes
home" but nobody ever says what it's like
to get on a plane for a three week tour
the elation of the first couple of audiences the good
feeling of exchange the running on the high
you get from singing good
and loud and long telling the world
what's on your mind

then comes the eighth show on the sixth day the beginning
to smell like the plane or bus the if-you-forget-your tooth-
    brush
in-one-spot-you-can't-brush-until-the-second-show the
    strangers
pulling at you cause they love you but you having no love
to give back
the singing the same songs night after night day after day
and if you read the gossip columns the rumors that your
    husband
is only after your fame

the wondering if your children will be glad to see you and
    maybe
the not caring if they are the scheming to get out
of just one show and go just one place where some doe-doe-
    dupaduke
won't say "just sing one song, please"

nobody mentions how it feels to become a freak
because you have talent and how
no one gives a damn how you feel
but only cares that aretha franklin is here like maybe that'll
stop:
                chickens from frying
                eggs from being laid
                crackers from hating
and if you say you're lonely or scared or tired how they
    always
just say "oh come off it" or "did you see
how much they loved you did you see huh did you?"
which most likely has nothing to do with you anyway
and i'm not saying aretha shouldn't have talent and i'm
    certainly
not saying she should quit
singing but as much as i love her i'd vote "yes" to her
doing four concerts a year and staying home or doing what-
    ever
she wants and making records cause it's a shame
the way we are killing her
we eat up artists like there's going to be a famine at the end
of those three minutes when there are in fact an abundance
of talents just waiting let's put some
of the giants away for a while and deal with them like they
    have
a life to lead

aretha doesn't have to relive billie holiday's life doesn't have
to relive dinah washington's death but who will
stop the pattern

she's more important than her music—if they must be
    separated—
and they should be separated when she has to pass out
    before

anyone recognizes she needs
a rest and i say i need
aretha's music
she is undoubtedly the one person who put everyone on
notice
she revived johnny ace and remembered lil green aretha
    sings
"i say a little prayer" and dionne doesn't
want to hear it anymore
aretha sings "money won't change you"
but james can't sing "respect" the advent
of aretha pulled ray charles from marlboro country
and back into
the blues made nancy wilson
try one more time forced
dionne to make a choice (she opted for the movies)
and diana ross had to get an afro wig pushed every
Black singer into Blackness and negro entertainers
into negroness you couldn't jive
when she said "you make me/feel" the blazers
had to reply "gotta let a man be/a man"
aretha said "when my show was in the lost and found/you
    came
along to claim it" and joplin said "maybe"
there has been no musician whom her very presence hasn't
affected when humphrey wanted her to campaign she said
"woeman's only hueman"
and he pressured james brown
they removed otis cause the combination was too strong
the impressions had to say "lord have mercy/we're moving
on up"
the Black songs started coming from the singers on stage
    and the dancers
in the streets
aretha was the riot was the leader if she had said "come
let's do it" it would have been done
temptations say why don't we think about it
                    think about it
                    think about it
                            1-21-'70

NO RESERVATIONS
(for Art Jones)

there are no reservations
for the revolution

no polite little clerk
to send notice
to your room
saying you are WANTED
on the battlefield

there are no banners
to wave you forward
no blaring trumpets
not even a blues note
moaning wailing lone blue note
to the yoruba drums saying
strike now   shoot
strike now   fire
strike now   run

there will be no grand
parade
and a lot thrown round
your neck
people won't look up and say
"why he used to live next to me
isn't it nice
it's his turn now"

there will be no recruitment
station
where you can give
the most convenient hours
"monday wednesday i play ball
friday night i play cards
any other time i'm free"
there will be no reserve
of energy
no slacking off till next time
"let's see— i can come back
next week

better not wear myself out
this time"

there will be reservations
only
if we fail

7-'69

ALONE

i can be
alone by myself
i was
lonely alone
now i'm lonely
with you
something is wrong
there are flies
everywhere
i go

8-'69

**THE GAME
OF GAME**

when all the cards are in
when all the chips are counted
the smiles smiled
the pictures taken
i wonder
if they'll say
you played a fair
game
of game?

2-19-'70

KIDNAP POEM

ever been kidnapped
by a poet
if i were a poet
i'd kidnap you
put you in my phrases and meter
you to jones beach
or maybe coney island
or maybe just to my house
lyric you in lilacs
dash you in the rain
blend into the beach
to complement my see
play the lyre for you
ode you with my love song
anything to win you
wrap you in the red Black green
show you off to mama
yeah if i were a poet i'd kid
nap you
                    2-17-'70

FOR A LADY OF PLEASURE
NOW RETIRED

some small island birthed
her and a big (probably) white ship took her
from mother to come
to america's recreation

she lives in the top of my building
i only know her through her eyes
she is old now not only from years
but from aging

one gets the impression she was most
beautiful and like good wine
or a semiprecious jewel touted out
for the pleasure of those
who could afford
her recreation

her head is always high
though the set of her mouth shows
it's not easy
she asks nothing
seems to have something
to give but no one to give it
to if ever she gave it
to anyone

age requires happy memories like louvenia smiled
when she died and though her doctor had told her not
to there was pork cooking
on the stove
there are so many new mistakes
for a lady of pleasure
that can be made it shouldn't be
necessary to repeat the old
ones

and it was cold
on the elevator that morning
when i spoke to her and foolishly asked
how are you

she smiled and tilted her head
      at least, i said, the sun is
      shining
and her eyes smiled   yes
and i was glad to be
there to say through spirits
      there is a new creation
to her
                        2-27-'70

2ND RAPP

they ain't gonna never get
rap
he's a note turned himself
into a million songs listen
to aretha call
his name

he's a light
turned himself into our homes
look how well we see
since he came

he's a spirit turned
pisces to aries
alpha to omega

he's a man
turned himself into Black
women
and we turn little hims
loose on the world
                        3-10-'70

A ROBIN'S POEM

if you plant grain
you get fields of flour
if you plant seeds
you get grass

or babies
i planted once
and a robin red breast flew
in my window
but a tom cat wouldn't let it
stay

TOY POEM

if they put you in a jack-in-the-box poet
would you pop up poeming a positive poem on
positive Blackness
would you poet a loving rawls poem and a real
st. jacques poem before they put them in a box

could you poet beyond the greek symbol into
the need for fraternity

if they put you in a wind up toy would you spin out liberated
woman
would you spin out a feminist or feminine
women have a different reality from men
would you spin into the arms of a Black man
or the clutch of white women

could you spin into an orphan home and liberate
a Black baby

if they took our insides out would we be still
Black people or would we become play toys
for master players
there's a reason we lose a lot it's not our game
and we don't know how to score

listen here
i wanna take you higher
5-25-'70

69

Everett Hoagland

PROLOGUE
~*Egyptian Remedy #4

Words to Drive out the White Growth in the Eyes

*(a formula to repeat over the brain of a tortoise that
is mixed in honey, and then laid on the eyes.)*

Who leads hither what he finds?

I lead forth what I find.
I lead forth your heads.
I lift up your necks.
I fasten what has been cut from you in its place.
I lead you forth to drive away the god of fevers
    and all possible deadly arts.

*   a Middle Kingdom Medical Recipe
     as adapted for *Technicians of the Sacred*
     from the "Papyrus of Ani"—the *Book of the Dead* 1500 B.C.

GEORGIA—IT'S THE GOSPEL TRUTH

I ain't seen the light
till I saw the night black ass
of Georgia White

talk!—
God in Jesus!

I ain't never seen a sight
till I checked the deep chocolate dawn
of Georgia spread out on sheets . . .
sweet sunshine in the middle of the night

hear me
Lord Jesus!!

But really y'all—

I ain't never had no way none of life
till I got to the hot ginger-bread
in the short drawers of Georgia White,
she got me coming like coconuts—

speak to the
Good God in Jesus!!—
(it's a terrible thing)

Lance Jeffers

WHEN SHE SPOKE OF GOD

Mrs. Williams' face was pleading when she spoke of her God to me,
but her God stood on tiptoe in her heart and could not reach
       the craggy monument of her love:
like a midget He craned futilely to see the fibre of her being
       as it stretched, an endless cloud, across her sky.

all gods touch the flesh of this giver and withdraw their
       frightened fingers,
bow to her footsteps on the dusty Alabama road

VIETNAM: I NEED MORE
THAN THIS CRUST OF SALT

I need more than this crust of salt upon my eye
       to thrust my dismay into the common street to beg for alms.
I need a switchblade in my pocket and an eye like the rumbler's
       on the block:
I need my switchblade to dissect the arteries of mass-murderers
       from whom I turn, trembling, ready for anyone,

for what task can I perform to wash the guilt from my skin,
       the thickness of the ice from the nation's eye?
What further rack can I mount for the stretching of my humanity,
       what kindness' platter place my head upon?
What stream of tears washing down the gutters of a ghetto
       will persuade the white man of the powdered-brick packed on
       his brain?
What rage of mine will clean the smokestack of his soul,
       deafen his ears to the butcher's song?

Keorapetse W. Kgositsile

WHEN BROWN IS BLACK
(For Rap Brown)

                    Are you not the light
                    that does not flicker
                    when murderers threaten summertime
                    passions of our time
                    Are you not the searchlight
                    in our eyes red with the dust
                    from the slave's empty grave
                    sending chills through
                    lynching johnsons around the world
                    as their obscene ghettos
                    go up in summertime flames

                    Some say it's youthful
                    adventure in the summertime
                    for they have lost natural instinct
                    which teaches a man to be free

                    "What does a penny buy?"

                    Are you not the fist
                    which articulates the passion
                    of the collective power of our rebirth
                    Are you not the fist
                    of the laughter of the rhythms
                    of the flames of our memory

                    "What does a penny buy?"

                    The naked head of the fuse
                    is up in the air pregnant
                    with the flaming children of our time
                    when Brown is Black
                    blowing up white myths
                    which built up layers of mists
                    which veiled the roads to the strength
                    of our laughter in the sun

But some
eating their balls in empty statements
say: it is youthful
adventure in the summertime

Now we said
the game is over, didn't we?
when we reach the end of the line
the shit goes up in flames, don't I say?

"What does a penny buy?"

For Malcolm,
for the brothers in Robben Island
for every drop of Black blood
        from every white whip
        from every white gun and bomb
for us and again for us
we shall burn
and beat the drum
resounding the bloodsong
from Sharpeville to Watts
and all points white of the memory
when the white game is over
and we dance to our bloodsong
without fear nor bales
.of tinted cotton over our eye

Go on, brother, say it. Talk
the talk slaves are afraid to live

"What does a penny buy?"
When Brown is Black

MANDELA'S SERMON

Blessed are the dehumanized
For they have nothing to lose
But their patience.

False gods killed the poet in me. Now
I dig graves
With artistic precision.

ELEGY FOR DAVID DIOP

He who thinks immortality
Flaming with furious fidelity
Could be dead has no head
You are the indignant air
Carrying fruit to nourish the continent
Unrelenting throbbing of the continent's heart
You are the dance and the dancer
The concrete foundation and the builder
Moving at lightning speed
Mating with fertile future
Refusing the touch of the stench
Of the carcass of rancid europe
I saw you explode
In Sharpeville burning
In Watts and the paddies
Of Vietnam and all dawn
Long I the desert palm
Drinking from your spring
Danced to the elegant
Replenishing of your majestic fire
Roaming the rhythms of your eternity
Because you are not a man
You are what Man should be
Eternal like the Word

IVORY MASKS IN ORBIT
(For Nina Simone)

these new night
babies flying on ivory wings
dig the beginning

do you love me!

son gawdamn
i saw the sun
rise at the midnight hour

300 sounds burn
on the ivory bespeaking
a new kind of air massive
as future memory

this like a finger moves
over 300 mississippis
rock the village
gates with future memory
of this moment's riff

the sun smiles of new
dawn mating with this
burning moment for the memory
can no longer kneel in

do you love me!

88 times over lovely
ebony lady swims in this
cloud like the crocodile
in the limpopo midnight
hour even here speaking
of love armed with future
memory: desire become memory
i know how you be tonight!

TO FANON

Tears,
hiding behind a doomed god
no longer define
the soul
because of your shock therapy
history's psychosis will be cured
once soft shack-born melodies explode
in love-loving hollers
in the womb of the future
exposing the shallow trenches
of make-belief history to the fury
of the midday sun
and now lovers weaving
their dreams into infinite
realities with ghetto charms will
with the light of the poet
show Jesus miracles

Etheridge Knight

HARD ROCK RETURNS TO PRISON FROM THE HOSPITAL FOR THE CRIMINAL INSANE

Hard Rock was "known not to take no shit
From nobody," and he had the scars to prove it:
Split purple lips, lumped ears, welts above
His yellow eyes, and one long scar that cut
Across his temple and plowed through a thick
Canopy of kinky hair.

The WORD was that Hard Rock wasn't a mean nigger
Anymore, that the doctors had bored a hole in his head,
Cut out part of his brain, and shot electricity
Through the rest. When they brought Hard Rock back,
Handcuffed and chained, he was turned loose,
Like a freshly gelded stallion, to try his new status.
And we all waited and watched, like indians at a corral,
To see if the WORD was true.

As we waited we wrapped ourselves in the cloak
Of his exploits: "Man, the last time, it took eight
Screws to put him in the Hole." "Yeah, remember when he
Smacked the captain with his dinner tray?" "He set
The record for time in the Hole—67 straight days!"
"Ol Hard Rock! man, that's one crazy nigger."
And then the jewel of a myth that Hard Rock had once bit
A screw on the thumb and poisoned him with syphilitic spit.

The testing came, to see if Hard Rock was really tame.
A hillbilly called him a black son of a bitch
And didn't lose his teeth, a screw who knew Hard Rock
From before shook him down and barked in his face.
And Hard Rock did *nothing*. Just grinned and looked silly,
His eyes empty like knot holes in a fence.

And even after we discovered that it took Hard Rock
Exactly 3 minutes to tell you his first name,
We told ourselves that he had just wised up,
Was being cool; but we could not fool ourselves for long,
And we turned away, our eyes on the ground. Crushed.

He had been our Destroyer, the doer of things
We dreamed of doing but could not bring ourselves to do,
The fears of years, like a biting whip,
Had cut grooves too deeply across our backs.

THE IDEA OF ANCESTRY

1

Taped to the wall of my cell are 47 pictures: 47 black
faces: my father, mother, grandmothers (1 dead), grand
fathers (both dead), brothers, sisters, uncles, aunts,
cousins (1st & 2nd), nieces, and nephews. They stare
across the space at me sprawling on my bunk. I know
their dark eyes, they know mine. I know their style,
they know mine. I am all of them, they are all of me;
they are farmers, I am a thief, I am me, they are thee.

I have at one time or another been in love with my mother,
1 grandmother, 2 sisters, 2 aunts (1 went to the asylum),
and 5 cousins. I am now in love with a 7 yr old niece
(she sends me letters written in large block print, and
her picture is the only one that smiles at me).

I have the same name as 1 grandfather, 3 cousins, 3 nephews,
and 1 uncle. The uncle disappeared when he was 15, just took
off and caught a freight (they say). He's discussed each year
when the family has a reunion, he causes uneasiness in
the clan, he is an empty space. My father's mother, who is 93
and who keeps the Family Bible with everybody's birth dates
(and death dates) in it, always mentions him. There is no
place in her Bible for "whereabouts unknown."

2

Each Fall the graves of my grandfathers call me, the brown
hills and red gullies of mississippi send out their electric
messages, galvanizing my genes. Last yr / like a salmon quitting
the cold ocean—leaping and bucking up his birthstream / I
hitchhiked my way from L.A. with 16 caps in my pocket and a
monkey on my back. and I almost kicked it with the kinfolks.

I walked barefooted in my grandmother's backyard/I smelled the
        old
land and the woods/I sipped cornwhiskey from fruit jars with the
        men/
I flirted with the women/I had a ball till the caps ran out
and my habit came down. That night I looked at my grandmother
and split/my guts were screaming for junk/but I was almost
contented/I had almost caught up with me.
(The next day in Memphis I cracked a croaker's crib for a fix.)

This yr there is a gray stone wall damming my stream, and when
the falling leaves stir my genes, I pace my cell or flop on my bunk
and stare at 47 black faces across the space. I am all of them,
they are all of me, I am me, they are thee, and I have no sons
to float in the space between.

AS YOU LEAVE ME

Shiny record albums scattered over
the livingroom floor, reflecting light
from the lamp, sharp reflections that hurt
my eyes as I watch you, squatting among the platters,
the beer foam making mustaches on your lips.

And, too,
the shadows on your cheeks from your long lashes
fascinate me—almost as much as the dimples:
in your cheeks, your arms and your legs:
dimples . . . dimples . . . dimples . . .

You
hum along with Mathis—how you love Mathis!
with his burnished hair and quicksilver voice that dances
among the stars and whirls through canyons
like windblown snow. sometimes I think that Mathis
could take you from me if you could be complete
without me. I glance at my watch. it is now time.

You rise,
silently, and to the bedroom and the paint:
on the lips red, on the eyes black,

and I lean in the doorway and smoke, and see you
grow old before my eyes, and smoke. why do you
chatter while you dress, and smile when you grab
your large leather purse? don't you know that when you
leave me I walk to the window and watch you? and light
a reefer as I watch you? and I die as I watch you
disappear in the dark streets
to whistle and to smile at the johns.

A LOVE POEM

I do not expect the spirit of Penelope
To enter your breast, for I am not mighty
Or fearless. (Only our love is brave,
A rock against the wind.) I cry and cringe
When the cyclops peers into my cave.

I do not expect your letters to be lengthy
And of love, flowery and philosophic, for
Words are not our bond.
I need only the hard fact
Of your existence for my subsistence.
Our love is a rock against the wind,
Not soft like silk and lace.

THE VIOLENT SPACE
(or when your sister sleeps around for money)

Exchange in greed the ungraceful signs. Thrust
The thick notes between green apple breasts.
Then the shadow of the devil descends,
The violent space cries and angel eyes,
Large and dark, retreat in innocence and in ice.
(Run sister run—the Bugga man comes!)

The violent space cries silently,
Like you cried wide years ago
In another space, speckled by the sun
And the leaves of a green plum tree,
And you were stung

81

By a red wasp and we flew home.
(Run sister run—the Bugga man comes!)

Well, hell, lil sis. wasps still sting.
You are all of seventeen and as alone now
In your pain as you were with the sting
On your brow.
Well, shit, lil sis, here we are:
You and I and this poem.
And what should I do? should I squat
In the dust and make strange markings on the ground?
Shall I chant a spell to drive the demon away?
(Run sister run—the Bugga man comes!)

In the beginning you were the Virgin Mary,
And you are the Virgin Mary now.
But somewhere between Nazareth and Bethlehem
You lost your name in the nameless void.
O Mary don't you weep don't you moan
O Mary shake your butt to the violent juke,
Absorb the demon puke and watch the white eyes pop.
(Run sister run—the Bugga man comes!)

And what do I do. I boil my tears in a twisted spoon
And dance like an angel on the point of a needle.
I sit counting syllables like Midas gold.
I am not bold. I can not yet take hold of the demon
And lift his weight from your black belly,
So I grab the air and sing my song.
(But the air can not stand my singing long.)

2 POEMS FOR BLACK RELOCATION CENTERS

I

Flukum couldn't stand the strain. Flukum
wanted inner and outer order, so
he joined the army where U.S. Manuals made
everything plain—even how to button his shirt,
and how to kill the yellow men. (If Flukum
ever felt hurt or doubt about who his enemy

was, the Troop Information Officer or the Stars
and Stripes straightened him out.)
Plus, we must not forget
that Flukum was paid well to let the Red
Blood. And sin? If Flukum ever thought about sin
or Hell for squashing the yellow men, the good Chaplain
(Holy by God and by Congress) pointed out with
Devilish skill that to kill the colored men was not
altogether a sin.

Flukum marched back from the war, straight and tall,
and with presents for all: a water pipe for daddy,
teeny tea cups for mama, sheer silk for tittee, and
a jade inlaid dagger for me. But, with a smile
on his face in a place just across the bay,
Flukum, the patriot, got shot that same day,
got shot in his great wide chest, bedecked with good
conduct ribbons. He died surprised, he had thought
the enemy far away on the other side of the sea.

(When we received his belongings they took away my dagger.)

II
Dead. He died in Detroit, his beard
was filled with lice; his halo glowed
and his white robe flowed magnificently
over the charred beams and splintered glass;
his stern blue eyes were rimmed with red,
and full of reproach; and the stench: roasted rats
and fat baby rumps swept up his nose that
had lost its arch of triumph. He died outraged,
and indecently, shouting impieties and betrayals.
And he arose out of his own ashes. Stripped.
A faggot in steel boots.

IT WAS A FUNKY DEAL

It was a funky deal.
The only thing real was red,
Red blood around his red, red beard.

It was a funky deal.

In the beginning was the word,
And in the end the deed.
Judas did it to Jesus
For the same Herd. Same reason.
You made them mad, Malcolm. Same reason.

It was a funky deal.

You rocked too many boats, man.
Pulled too many coats, man.
Saw through the jive.
You reached the wild guys
Like me. You and Bird. (And that
Lil LeRoi cat.)

It was a **Funky** deal.

THE SUN CAME

And if sun comes
How shall we greet him?
            —Gwendolyn Brooks

            The Sun came, Miss Brooks,—
            After all the night years.
            He came spitting fire from his lips.
            And we flipped—We goofed the whole thing.
            It looks like our ears were not equipped
            For the fierce hammering.

            And now the Sun has gone, has bled red,
            Weeping behind the hills.
            Again the night year shadows form.
            But beneath the placid faces a storm rages.
            The rays of Red have pierced the deep, have struck
            The core. We cannot sleep.
            The shadows sing: Malcolm, Malcolm, Malcolm.

            The Sun came, Miss Brooks.
            And we goofed the whole thing.
            I think.
            (Though ain't no vision visited my cell).

Don L. Lee

"STEREO"

I can clear a beach or swimming pool without
        touching water.
I can make a lunch counter become deserted
        in less than an hour.
I can make property value drop by being seen
        in a realtor's tower.
I ALONE can make the word of God have little
        or no meaning to many
        in Sunday morning's prayer hour.
I have Power,
BLACK POWER.

AWARENESS

BLACK	PEOPLE	THINK
PEOPLE	BLACK	PEOPLE
THINK	PEOPLE	THINK
BLACK	PEOPLE	THINK—
THINK	BLACK.	

THE CURE ALL

The summer is
coming.

CONGRESS HAS ACTED:

money into the
ghetto,

to keep the weather
cool.

THE NEW INTEGRATIONIST

I

seek

integration

of

negroes

with

black

people.

TWO POEMS
(from "Sketches from a Black-Nappy-Headed Poet")

last week
my mother died/
& the most often asked question
at the funeral
was not of her death
or of her life before death
                            but
why was i present
with/out
a
tie on.

i ain't seen no poems stop a .38,
i ain't seen no stanzas brake a honkie's head,
i ain't seen no metaphors stop a tank,
i ain't seen no words kill
& if the word was mightier than the sword
pushkin wouldn't be fertilizing russian soil/
& until my similes can protect me from a night stick
i guess i'll keep my razor
& buy me some more bullets.

PAINS WITH A LIGHT TOUCH
(for my middle class friends
with their spit-level homes
and lives)

He was married
for a short time,

Too long.

His marriage was not completely in pain,
He learned many things from his wife—
Instructive things, such as, to talk on the phone
        for hours, without saying something, to view
        TV, listen to radio & sleep at the same time,
        how to wish the dishes washed, how to be the
        best dressed, brokest employee at work, how to
        have nothing yet think you possess something or
        have something and possess nothing, how to com-
        plete the full text of Orwell's "Animal Farm"
        in less than a year and say it was about pigs,
        how to clean the house while dancing, how
        to cleverly sweep the rug under the dirt and
        how to make laziness into a virtue.

His mind was greatly improved
when she told him that Yevtushenko
was a Russian salad and
                        supposedly tasted good.

After trying to buy some,
                he continued to
        rationalize his observations.

Success was his until a friend
asked him about his poetry
and he started talking about
chickens.

He left home, again—
Happy and vowed to stay

Happy.

IN THE INTEREST OF BLACK SALVATION

Whom can I confess to?
The Catholics have some cat
They call father,
                    mine cutout a long time ago—
Like His did.
I tried confessing to my girl,
But she is not fast enough—except on hair styles,
                                        clothes
                                        face care and
                                        television.
If ABC, CBS, and NBC were to become educational stations
She would probably lose her cool,
                            and learn to read
Comic Books.
My neighbor, 36-19-35 volunteered to listen but
I couldn't talk—
Her numbers kept getting in the way,
Choking me.
To a Buddhist friend I went.
Listen, he didn't—
Advise, he did.
        "pray, pray, pray, and keep one eye open."
I didn't pray—kept both eyes open.

Visited three comrades at Fort Hood,
There are no Cassandra cries here,
No one would hear you anyway. They didn't.
Three tried to speak, "don't want to make war."
                                    why???

When you could do countless other things like
Make life, this would be—
Useless too . . .

When I was 17,
I didn't have time to dream,
Dreams didn't exist—
Prayers did, as dreams.
I am now 17 & 8,

I still don't dream.
Father forgive us for we know what we do.
Jesus saves,
            Jesus saves,
                        Jesus saves—S & H Green Stamps.

THE WALL
(43rd & Langley, Chicago, Ill.
painted by the artists and
photographers of OBAC 8/67)

sending their negro
toms into the ghetto
at all hours of the day
(disguised as black people)
to dig
the wall, (the weapon)
the mighty black wall (we chase them out—kill if necessary)

whi-te people can't stand
the wall,
killed their eyes, (they cry)
black beauty hurts them—
they thought black beauty was a horse—
stupid muthafuckas, they run from
the mighty black wall

brothers & sisters screaming,
"picasso ain't got shit on us.
send him back to art school"
we got black artists
who paint black art
the mighty black wall

negroes from south shore &
hyde park coming to check out
a black creation
black art, of the people,
for the people,
art for people's sake
black people
the mighty black wall

black photographers
who take black pictures
can you dig,
            blackburn
            le roi,
            muslim sisters,
                    black on gray it's hip
they deal, black photographers deal blackness for
the mighty black wall

black artists paint,
            du bois/ garvey/ gwen brooks
            stokely/ rap/ james brown
            trane/ miracles/ ray charles
            baldwin/ killens/ muhammad ali
            alcindor/ blackness/ revolution
our heros, we pick them, for the wall
the mighty black wall/ about our business, blackness
                            can you dig?
if you can't you ain't black/ some other color
negro maybe?

the wall,
the mighty black wall,
"ain't the muthafucka layen there?"

THE DEATH DANCE
(for Maxine)

            my empty steps mashed
            your face in a mad
            rhythm of happiness.
            as if i was just learning to
            boo-ga-loo

            my mother took the
            'b' train to the loop
            to seek work & was laughed at by
            some dumb, eye-less image maker as
            she scored idiot on "your" I.Q. test.

90

i watched mom;
an ebony mind
on a yellow frame.
"i got work son, go back to school."
(she was placed according to her
intelligence into some honkie's kitchen)

i thought & my steps
took on a hip be-bop beat
on your little brain
trying to reach any of
your senseless senses.

mom would come home late
at night & talk sadtalk
or funny sadtalk. she talked
about a pipe smoking sissy
who talked sissy-talk & had
sissy sons who were forever playing
sissy games with themselves
& then she would say,
"son you is a man, a black man."

i was now tapdancing on your
balls & you felt no pain.
my steps were beating a staccato
message that told of the past 400 years.

the next day mom cried &
sadtalked me. she talked about
the eggs of maggot colored,
gaunt creatures from europe
who came here/ put on pants, stopped eating with their hands
stole land, massacred indians,
hid from the sun, enslaved blacks &
thought that they were substitutes
for gods. she talked about a
faggot who grabbed her ass as
she tried to get out of the
backdoor of his kitchen & she said,
"son you is a man, a black man."

the African ballet
was now my guide; a teacher of self &

the dance of a people.
a dance of concept & essence.
i grew.

mom stayed home & the
ADC became my father/ in projects without
backdoors/ "old grand dad" over
the cries of bessie smith /
until pains didn't pain anymore.

i began to dance dangerous steps,
warrior's steps.
my steps took on a cadence with other blk/brothers
& you could hear the cracking of
gun shots in them & we said that,
"we were men, black men."

i took the 'b' train to the loop &
you SEE me coming,
you don't like it,
you can't hide &
you can't stop me.
you will not laugh this time.
you know
that when i dance again
it will be the
Death Dance.

BUT HE WAS COOL
or: he even stopped for green lights

super-cool
ultrablack
a tan/purple
had a beautiful shade.

he had a double-natural
that wd put the sisters to shame.
his dashikis were tailor made
& his beads were imported sea shells
    (from some blk/country i never heard of)
he was triple-hip.

his tikis were hand carved
out of ivory
& came express from the motherland.
he would greet u in swahili
& say good-by in yoruba.
woooooooooooo-jim he bes so cool & ill tel li gent
        cool-cool is so cool he was un-cooled by
            other niggers' cool
        cool-cool ultracool was bop-cool/ice box
            cool so cool cold cool
        his wine didn't have to be cooled, him was
            air conditioned cool
        cool-cool/real cool made me cool—now
            ain't that cool
        cool-cool so cool him nick-named refrigerator.

cool-cool so cool
he didn't know,
after detroit, newark, chicago &c.,
we had to hip
        cool-cool/ super-cool/ real cool
  that
to be black
is
to be
very-hot.

DON'T CRY, SCREAM
(for John Coltrane/ from a black poet/
in a basement apt. crying dry tears
of "you ain't gone.")
        into the sixties
        a trane
        came/ out of the
        fifties with a
        golden boxcar
        riding the rails
        of novation.
            blowing
            a-melodics
            screeching,
            screaming,

blasting—
> driving some away,
> (those paper readers who thought
> manhood was something innate)
>
> bring others in,
> (the few who didn't believe that the
> world existed around established whi
> teness & leonard bernstein)

music that ached.
murdered our minds (we reborn)
born into a neoteric aberration.
& suddenly
you envy the
BLIND man—
you know that he will
hear what you'll never
see.
> your music is like
> my head—nappy black/
> a good nasty feel with
> tangled songs of:

we-eeeeeeeeee	sing
WE-EEEeeeeeeeeee	loud &
WE-EEEEEEEEEEEEEEEE	high
	with
	feeling

a people playing
the sound of me when
i combed it. combed at
it.

i cried for billie holiday.
the blues. we ain't blue
the blues exhibited illusions of manhood.
destroyed by you. Ascension into:

scream-eeeeeeeeeeeeee-ing	sing
SCREAM-EEEeeeeeeeeeee-ing	loud &
SCREAM-EEEEEEEEEEEEEE-ing	long with
	feeling

we ain't blue, we are black.
we ain't blue, we are black.
                    (all the blues did was
                    make me cry)
soultrane gone on a trip
he left man images
he was a life-style of
man-makers & annihilator
of attache case carriers.

Trane done went.
(got his hat & left me one)
naw brother,
i didn't cry,
i just—
        Scream-eeeeeeeeeeeeee-ed   sing loud
        SCREAM-EEEEEEEEEEEEEEEEEE-ED   & high with
          we-eeeeeeeeeeeeeeeeeeeeee ee   feeling
          WE-EEEEEEeeeeeeeeeEEEEEEEE   letting
          WE-EEEEEEEEEEEEEEEEEEEEEEE   yr/voice
          WHERE YOU DONE GONE, BROTHER?break

it hurts, grown babies
dying. born. done caught me
a trane. steel wheels broken
by popsicle sticks. i went out
& tried to buy a nickle bag
with my standard oil card.

                    (swung on a faggot who politely
                    scratched his ass in my presence.
                    he smiled broken teeth stained from
                    his over-used tongue. fisted-face.
                    teeth dropped in tune with ray
                    charles singing "yesterday.")

blonds had more fun—
with snagga-tooth niggers
who saved pennies & pop bottles for weekends
to play negro & other filthy inventions.
be-bop-en to james brown's
cold sweat—these niggers didn't sweat,

they perspired. & the blond's dye came out,
i ran. she did too, with his pennies, pop bottles
& his mind. tune in next week same time same station
for anti-self in one lesson.

to the negro cow-sissies
who did tchaikovsky &
the beatles & live in
split-level homes & had
split level minds & babies.
who committed the act of
love with their clothes on.
                    (who hid in the bathroom to read
                    jet mag., who didn't read the chicago
                    defender because of the misspelled
                    words & had shelves of books by
                    europeans on display. untouched. who
                    hid their little richard & lightnin'
                    slim records & asked: "John who?")

                    instant hate.)
they didn't know any better,
brother, they were too busy getting
into debt, expressing humanity &
taking off color.

        SCREAMMMM/we-eeeee/screech/teee   improvise
        aheeeeeeeee/screeeeeee/theeee/ee   with
        ahHHHHHHHHH/WEEEEEEEE/scrEEE   feeling
            EEEE
        we-eeeeeeWE-EEEEEEEEWE-EE-EEEEE
the ofays heard you &
were wiped out. spaced.
one clown asked me during,
my favorite things, if
you were practicing.
i fired on the muthafucka & said,
"i'm practicing."

naw brother,
i didn't cry.
i got high off my thoughts—
they kept coming back,
back to destroy me.

96

& that BLIND man
i don't envy him anymore
i can see his hear
& hear his heard through my pores.
i can see my me. it was truth you gave,
like a daily shit
it had to come.

                can you scream—brother?   very
                can you scream—brother?   soft

i hear you.
i hear you.

and the Gods will too.

ASSASSINATION

            it was wild.
            the
            bullet hit high.
                        (the throat-neck)
            & from everywhere:
                    the motel, from under bushes and cars,
                    from around corners and across streets,
                    out of the garbage cans and from rat holes
                    in the earth
            they came running.
            with
            guns
            drawn
            they came running
        toward the King—
                    all of them
                    fast and sure—
            as if
            the King
            was going to fire back.
            they came running,
            fast and sure,
            in the
            wrong
            direction.

MALCOLM SPOKE/ WHO LISTENED?
(this poem is for my consciousness too)

he didn't say
wear yr/blackness in
outer garments
& blk/slogans fr/the top 10.

he was fr a long
line of super-cools,
        doo-rag lovers &
        revolutionary pimps.
u are playing that
high-yellow game in blackface
minus the straighthair.
now
it's nappy-black
& air conditioned volkswagens
with undercover whi
te girls who studied faulkner at
smith
& are authorities on "militant"
knee/grows
selling u at jew town rates:
        niggers with wornout tongues
        three for a quarter/ or will consider a trade

the double-breasted hipster
has been replaced with a
dashiki wearing rip-off
who went to city college
majoring in physical education.

animals come in all colors.
dark meat will roast as fast as whi-te meat
especially in
the unitedstatesofamerica's
new
self-cleaning ovens.

if we don't listen.

A POEM TO COMPLEMENT OTHER POEMS

change.
like if u were a match i wd light u into something beauti-
      ful. change.
change.
for the better into a realreal together thing. change, from
      a make believe
nothing on corn meal and water. change.
change. from the last drop to the first, maxwellhouse
      did. change.
change was a programmer for IBM, thought him was a
      brown computor. change.
colored is something written on southern out-
      houses. change.
greyhound did, i mean they got rest rooms on buses.
      change.
change.
change nigger.
saw a nigger hippy, him wanted to be different. changed.
saw a nigger liberal, him wanted to be different.
      changed.
saw a nigger conservative, him wanted to be different.
      changed.
niggers don't u know that niggers are different. change.
a doublechange. nigger wanted a double zero in front of
      his name; a license to kill,
niggers are licensed to be killed. change. a negro: some-
      thing pigs eat.
change. i say change into a realblack righteous aim. like
      i don't play
saxophone but that doesn't mean i don't dig 'trane.'
      change.
change.
hear u coming but yr/steps are too loud. change. even a
      lamp post changes nigger.
change, stop being an instant yes machine. change.
niggers don't change they just grow. that's a change;
      bigger & better niggers.

change, into a necessary blackself.
change, like a gas meter gets higher.
change, like a blues song talking about a righteous to-
        morrow.
change, like a tax bill getting higher.
change, like a good sister getting better.
change, like knowing wood will burn. change.
know the realenemy.
change,
change nigger: standing on the corner, thought him was
            cool. him still
        standing there. it's winter time, him cool.
change,
know the realenemy.
change: him wanted to be a TV star. him is. ten o'clock
            news.
        wanted, wanted. nigger stole some lemon & lime
            popsicles,
        thought them were diamonds.
change nigger change.
know the realenemy.
change: is u is or is u aint. change. now now change. for
        the better change.
        read a change. live a change. read a blackpoem.
            change. be the realpeople.
        change. blackpoems
will change:
know the realenemy. change. know the realenemy. change
        yr/enemy change know the real
change know the realenemy change, change, know the
        realenemy, the realenemy, the real
realenemy change your the enemies / change your change
        your change your enemy change
your enemy. know the realenemy, the world's enemy.
        know them know them know them the
realenemy change your enemy change your change
        change change your enemy change change
change change your change change change.
your
mind nigger.

BLACKMUSIC / A BEGINNING

pharoah sanders
had
finished
playing
&
the whi-
te boy was to
go on next.

him didn't

him sd
that
his horn
was
broke.

they sat
there
dressed in
african garb
& dark sun glasses
listening to the brothers
play.   (taking notes)
we
didn't realize
who they
were un
til their
next recording
had been
released: the beach boys play soulmusic.
real sorry about
the supremes
being dead,
heard some whi
te girls
the other day—
all wigged-down
with a mean tan—

soundin just like them,
singin
rodgers & hart
& some country & western.

BLACKWOMAN

blackwoman:
is an
in and out
rightsideup
action-image
of her man . . . .
in other
(blacker) words;
she's together,
if
he
bes.

THE REVOLUTIONARY SCREW
(for my blacksisters)

brothers,
i
under/overstand
the situation:

i mean—
        u bes hitten the man hard
        all day long.
a stone revolutionary, "a full time revolutionary."
        tellen the man how bad u is
        & what u goin ta do
        & how u goin ta do it.

it must be a bitch
to be able to do all that
talken. (& not one irregular breath fr/yr/mouth)
being so
forceful & all
to the man's face (the courage)
& u not even cracken a smile (realman).

i know,
the sisters just don't
understand the
pressure u is under.

&
when u ask for a piece
of leg/
it's not for yr/self
but for
yr/people————it keeps u going
& anyway u is a revolutionary
& she wd be doin
a revolutionary thing.

that sister dug it
from the beginning,
had an early-eye.
i mean
she really had it together
when she said:
            go fuck yr/self nigger.

now
that was
revolutionary.

REFLECTIONS ON A LOST LOVE
(for my brothers who think they are lovers
and my sisters who are the real-lovers)

            back in chi/
            all the blackwomen
            are fine,

super fine.
even the ones who:
      dee bob/de bop/ she-shoo-bop
      bop de-bop/ dee dee bop/ dee-she dee-she-bop
      we—We eeeeeeeeeeeeeee/ WEEEEEEEEEEEEEEE
they so fine/
that
when i slide up
                to one & say: take it off   sing
                              take it off   slow
                                      take it all off   with feeling
& she would say: "if i doos,
              does us think u can groove dad———dy"
& i wd say: "can chitlins smell,
           is toejam black,
           can a poet, poet,
           can a musician, music?"

              weeeee/weeeeeee/de-bop-a-dee-bop
              whooo-bop/dee-bop a-she-bop
as she smiled
& unbuttoned that top button
i sd: take it off   sing
          take it off   slow
              take it all off   with feeling
first the skirt,
then the blouse
& next her wig (looked like she made it herself)
next the shoes & then
the eyelashes and jewelry
&
      dee-bop/ bop-a-ree-bop/ WOW
the slip
& next the bra (they weren't big, but that didn't scare me)
cause i was grooven now: dee/ dee-bop-a-she-bop/
      weeeeeEEEEEEEEEE
as she moved to the most important part,
i got up & started to groove myself but my eyes stopped
      me.
first
her stockens down those shapely legs—
followed by black bikini panties, that just slid down

and
i just stood—
& looked with utter amazement as she said: in a deep
              "hi baby—my name is   man-like
              joe sam."   voice

A POEM LOOKING FOR A READER
(to be read with a love consciousness)

        black is not
        all inclusive,
        there are other colors.
        color her warm and womanly,
        color her feeling and life,
        color her a gibran poem & 4 women of simone.
        children will give her color
        paint her the color of her
        man.

        most of all color her
        love
        a remembrance of life
        a truereflection
        that we
        will
        move   u will move with
        i want
        u
        a fifty minute call to blackwomanworld:
                hi baby,
                how u doin?
        need u.
        listening to
        young-holt's, *please sunrise, please.*

        to give   i'll give
        most personal.
        what about the other
        scenes: children playing in vacant lots,
                or like the first time u knowingly kissed a girl,
                was it joy or just beautifully beautiful.

i
remember at 13
reading chester himes'
cast the first stone and
the eyes of momma when she caught me: read on, son.

how will u come:
        like a soulful strut in a two-piece beige o-rig'i-nal,
        or afro-down with a beat in yr/walk?
how will love come:
        painless and deep like a razor cut
        or like some cheap 75¢ movie;
        i think not.

will she be the woman
other men will want
or
will her beauty be
accented with my name on it?

she will come as she would
want her man to come.
she'll come,
she'll come.
i
never wrote a love letter
but
that doesn't mean
i
don't love.

A MESSAGE ALL BLACKPEOPLE CAN DIG
(& a few negroes too)

        we are going to do it.
        US: blackpeople, beautiful people; the sons and daugh-
                ters of beautiful people.

bring it back to
US: the unimpossibility.
now is
the time, the test
while there is something to save (other than our lives).

we'll move together
hands on weapons & families
blending into the sun,
into each/other.
we'll love,
we've always loved.
just be cool & help one/another.
go ahead.
walk a righteous direction
under the moon,
in the night
bring new meanings to
the north star,
the blackness,
to US.

discover new stars:
street-light stars that will explode into evil-eyes,
light-bulb stars visible only to the realpeople,
clean stars, african & asian stars,
black aesthetic stars that will damage the whi-temind;
killer stars that will move against
the unpeople.

come
brothers/fathers/sisters/mothers/sons/daughters
dance as one
walk slow & hip.
hip to what life is
and can be.
& remember we are not hippies,
WE WERE BORN HIP.
walk on. smile a little
yeah, that's it beautiful people
move on in, take over. take over, take over take/over
            takeovertakeover overtakeovertakeovertake over/

                        take over take, over take,
                    over take, over take.
        blackpeople
        are moving, moving to return
                    this earth into the hands of
        human beings.

MIXED SKETCHES

u feel that way sometimes
wondering:
as a nine year old sister
with burned out hair oddly
smiles at you and sweetly calls you
brother.

u feel that way sometimes
wondering:
as a blackwoman & her 6 children
are burned out of their apartment with no place
to go & a nappy-headed nigger comes running thru
our neighborhood with a match in his hand cryin
revolution.

u feel that way sometimes
wondering:
seeing sisters in two hundred dollar wigs & suits
fastmoving in black clubs in late surroundings   talking
about late thoughts in late language waiting for late men
that come in with, "i don't want to hear bout nothing black
        tonight."

u feel that way sometimes
wondering:
while eating on newspaper tablecloths
& sleeping on clean bed sheets that couldn't
stop bed bugs   as black children watch their
mothers leave the special buses returning from
special neighborhoods
to clean their "own" unspecial homes.
u feel that way sometimes
wondering:
wondering, how did we survive?

ON SEEING DIANA GO MADDDDDDDDD

(on the very special occasion of the death of her two dogs—
Tiffany & Li'l Bit—when she cried her eyelashes off)

a dog lover,
a lover of dogs in a land where poodles
eat/live cleaner than their masters
& their masters use the colored people
to walk that which they love, while they
wander in & out of our lives running the world.

(stop! in the name of love, before you break my heart)

u moved with childlike vision
deeper into lassieland to become
the new wonderwoman of the dirty-world
we remember the 3/ the three young baaaaaad detroiters
of younger years when i & other blacks moved with u
& all our thoughts dwelled on the limits of forget & forgive.

(stop! in the name of love, before you break my heart)

diana,
we left u (back in those un-thinking days)   there
on the dance floor teaching marlon brando the monkey
(the only dance you performed with authority)
we washed our faces anew
as the two of you dreamed a single mind.
diana,
yr/new vision worries me because i,
as once you, knew/know the hungry days   when
our fathers went to ford motor co.,
and our mothers
in the morning traffic to the residential sections of dearborn.
little surpreme, only the well fed *forget.*

(stop! in the name of love, before you break . . . . .)

ladies & gents we proudly present
the swinging sur-premessssss . . . . correction, correction.
ladies & gents we proudly present
diana rossss and the surpremes.

and there u stood,
a skinny earthling viewing herself as a mov
ing star. as a mov   ing star u will travel
north by northwest deeper into the ugliness
of yr/bent ego. & for this i/we cannot forgive.

stop! in the name of love, ...)

u the gifted voice, a symphony, have now joined the
hippy generation to become unhipped,
to become the symbol of a new aberration,
the wearer of other people's hair.
to become one of the real animals of this earth.
we wish u luck & luckily u'll need it
in yr/new found image of a mov
ing star, a mov   ing star, mov   ing moving
moving on to play
a tooth-pick in a *rin tin tin* mov   ie.

A POEM FOR A POET
(for brother Mahmood Darweesh)

read yr/exile
i had a mother too,
& her death will not be
talked of around the world.
like you,
i live/walk a strange land.
my smiles are real but seldom.

our enemies eat the same bread
and their waste
(there is always waste)
is given to the pigs,
and then they consume the pigs.

Africa still has sun & moon,
has clean grass & water u can see thru;
Africa's people talk to u with their whole faces,
and their speech comes like drumbeats, comes like drumbeats.

our enemies eat the same bread
and the waste from their greed
will darken your sun and hide your moon,
will dirty your grass and mis-use your water.
your people will talk with unchanging eyes
and their speech will be slow & unsure & overquick.

Africa, be yr/ own letters
or
all your people will want cars
and there are few roads.
you must eat yr/own food
and that which is left,
continue to share in earnest.

Keep your realmen; yr/sculptors
yr/ poets, yr/fathers, yr/musicians, yr/sons, yr/warriors.
Keep your truemen of the darkskin,
a father guides his children,
keep them & they'll return your wisdom,
and
if you must send them,   send them
the way of the Sun
as to make them

blacker.

CHANGE IS NOT ALWAYS PROGRESS
(for Africa & Africans)

Africa.

don't let them
steal
your face   or
take your circles
and make them squares.

don't let them
steel
your body   as to put
100 stories of concrete on you

so that you
                    arrogantly
      scrape
      the

      sky.

FOR BLACK PEOPLE

*(& negroes too. a poetic statement on black existence in
america with a view of tomorrow. all action takes place on
the continent of north america. these words, imperfect as they
may be, are from positive images received from gwendolyn
brooks, hoyt w. fuller, imamu baraka & joe goncalves.)*

I: IN THE BEGINNING

state street was dead. wiped out.
ghetto expressways were up-lifted
and dropped on catholic churches.
all around us trees were being up rooted.
and flung into the entrances of bars, taverns & houses
of prostitution
lake meadows and prairie shores
passed our faces with human bodies of
black & whi-te mixed together, like salt & pepper,
—in concrete silence.
though deceased, some of the bodies still had smiles
—on their faces.
BONG BONG BONG BONG BONG BONG BONG
        BONG
IT STARTED LAST SUNDAY.
for some unknown reason all the baptist ministers—
        told the truth.
it was like committing mass suicide.
it was cold, mid-december, but the streets were hot.
the upward bound programs had failed that year.
the big bombs had been dropped, harlem &
        newark were annihilated.
another six million had perished and now

the two big men were fighting for universal survival.
the scene was blow for blow at the corner of 59th & racine,
right in front of the "Lead Me By the Hand"
        storefront church.
J.C., the blue eyed blond, had the upper hand for his
opponent, Allah, was weakening because of the strange—
        climate.
ahhhhh, ohoooooo, ahhaaaaa, ahhhaaaeeEEEE
in a bedroom across the street a blk/woman tearlessly
cries as she spread her legs, in hatred, for her landlord—
        paul goldstein.
(her children will eat tonight)
her brothers, boy-men called negroes, were off hiding
in some known place biting their nails & dreaming of
        whi-te virgins.
that year negroes continued to follow blind men whose
        eye-vision was less than their own & each morning
        negroes woke up a little deader.
the sun was less than bright, air pollution acted as a filter.
colored people were fighting each other knowingly
and little niggers were killing little niggers.
the "best" jobs were taken by colored college graduates
who had earned their degrees in a four year course of
        self-hatred with a minor in speech.
negroes religiously followed a blondhairedblueeyedman
        and no one forced them
whi-te boys continued to laugh and take blk/women.
negroes were unable to smile & their tears were dry. They
        had no eye-balls.
their sisters went to strangers' beds cursing them.
that year negroes read styron, mailer, joyce and rimbaud.
last year it was bellow, wallace, sartre & voznesensky
(yevtushenko was unpoetic).
somebody said that there was no such thing as black lit-
erature & anyway we all knew that negroes didn't write,
except occasional letters to the editor.
niggers 3 steps from being shoeshine boys were dressing
and talking like william buckley jr.—minus the pencil.
their heroes danced unclothed out of greek mythology.

janis smyth & claude iforgethislastname often quoted pas-
    sages from antigone (pronounced anti-gone).
the pope, all perfumed down—smelling like a french sissy,
watched 59th and racine from st. peters with a rosary
    in his hand:
                    hell mary full of grace the lord is with thee.
                    hell mary full of grace the lord is with thee.
                    hell mary full of grace the lord was with thee.
blk/ poets were not citizens & were being imprisoned and
    put to death.
whi-te boys remained our teachers & taught the people
    of color
how to be negroes and homosexuals.
some invisible fiction writer continued to praise the pov-
    erty program & is now being considered for "negro
    writer in residence" at johnson city, texas.
a blind negro poet compared himself with yeats
not knowing that he, himself, was a "savage side show."
all this happened in the beginning
and the beginning is almost the end.

II. TRANSITION AND MIDDLE PASSAGE

gas masks were worn as were side-arms.
the two nations indivisible & black people began to believe
    in themselves.
muhammad ali remained the third world's champ &
    taught the people self defense.
blk/poets were released from prison & acted as consult-
    ants to the blk/nation.
there were regular napalm raids over the whi-te house.
college trained negroes finally realized that they weren't
    educated and expressed sorrow for losing their virginity
    in europe.
the urban progress centers were transformed into hospitals
    & the records were used for toilet paper.
the room was whi-te & the blacks entered only to find
    that the two colors wouldn't mix.
deee-bop a bop bop, dee dee abop, bop-o-bop dee dee,
    wee, WEEEEEE.
willie johnson, all processed down, was noticeably driving
down cottage grove in a gold & black deuce & a quarter;

hitting the steering wheel at 60 degrees off center, with
his head almost touching the right window. willie, dressed
in a gold ban-lon that matched his ride, slowly moved his
left foot to his dual stereo that coolly gave out jerry
butler's: "never gone ta give you up."
while miss wilberforce, alias miss perm of 1967, tried
to pass him on his right side in her pine-yellow 287 must-
ang with the gas tank always on full, dressed in a two
piece beige marshall field's o-ri-ginal, miss perm with·hair
flowing in the wind was nodding her head to the same
tune:
     "never gone ta give you up."
both, the stang & the deuce hit the corner of 39th & cottage
at the same time; and as if somebody said, "black is
beautiful," miss perm and processed-down looked at each
other with educated eyes that said:
              i hate you.
that year even lovers didn't love.
whi-te boys continued to take blk/women to bed; but they
     ceased to wake up alive.
this was the same year that the picture "Guess Who's
     Coming to Dinner" killed spencer tracy.
negro pimps were perpetual victims of assassination &
     nobody cried.
Amiri Baraka wrote the words to the blk/national anthem &
     pharoah sanders composed the music. tauhid became
     our war song.
an alive wise man will speak to us, he will quote du bois,
nkrumah, coltrane, fanon, muhammad, trotter and him-
     self. we will listen.
chicago became known as negro-butcher to the world &
     no one believed it would happen, except the jews—the
     ones who helped plan it.
forgetting their own past—they were americans now.
eartha kitt talked to nbc about blk/survival; receiving
     her instructions from the bedroom at night.
blk/people stopped viewing TV & received the new
     messages from the talking drum.
dope pushers were given over doses of their own junk
     & they died. no one cried.
united fruit co. & standard oil were wiped out & whi-te
     people cried.

at last, the president could not control our dreams
and the only weapon he could threaten us with
        was death.

III. THE END IS THE REAL WORLD

it is a new day and the sun is not dead.
Allah won the fight at 59th & racine and his sons are not
        dead.
blk/poets are playing & we can hear. marvin x & Askia
Muhammad Touré walk the streets with smiles on their
faces. i join them. we talk & listen to our own words.
we set aside one day a year in remembrance of whi-teness.
                        (anglo-saxon american history day)
the air is clean. men & women are able to love.
legal holidays still fall in february: the 14th and 23rd*.
all the pigs were put to death, the ones with men-like
        minds too.
men stopped eating each other and hunger existed only in
        history books.
money was abolished and everybody was rich.
every home became a house of worship & pure water runs
        again.
young blk/poets take direction from older blk/poets &
        everybody listens.
those who speak have something to say & people seldom
        talk about themselves.
those who have something to say wait their turn & listen to
        their own message.
the hip thing is not to be cool & get high but to be cool &
        help yr/brother.
the pope retired & returned the land & valuables his
        organization had stolen under the guise of religion.
Allah became a part of the people & the people knew &
        loved him as they knew and loved themselves.
the world was quiet and gentle and beauty came back.
people were able to breathe.
blk/women were respected and protected & their actions

---

*Birth dates of Frederick Douglass and W.E.Du Bois

proved deserving of such respect & protection.
each home had a library that was overused.
the blackman had survived.
he was truly the "desert people."
there were black communities, red communities, yellow
        communities and a few whi-te communities that were
        closely watched.
there was not a need for gun control.
there was no need for the word peace for its
        antonym had been removed from the vocabulary.
like i sd befo
the end is the real world.

                                            July, 1968

MOVE UN-NOTICED TO BE NOTICED:
A NATIONHOOD POEM

move, into our own, not theirs
into our.
they own it (for the moment):   the unclean world, the
                                 polluted space, the un-censor-
                                 ed air, yr/foot steps as they
                                 run wildly in the wrong
                                 direction.
move, into our own, not theirs
into our.
move, you can't buy own.
own is like yr/hair (if u let it live); a natural extension of
        ownself.
own is yr/reflection, yr/total-being; the way u walk, talk,
                    dress and relate to each other is *own*.

own is you,
cannot be bought or sold: can u buy yr/writing hand
                           yr/dancing feet, yr/speech,
                           yr/woman (if she's real),
                           yr/manhood?
own is ours.
all we have to do is   *take it,*
take it the way u take from one another,

the way u take artur rubenstein over thelonious
monk,
the way u take eugene genovese over lerone bennett,
the way u take robert bly over imamu baraka,
the way u take picasso over charles white,
the way u take marianne moore over gwendolyn
brooks,
the way u take *inaction* over *action.*

move. move to act.   act.
act into thinking and think into action.
try to think. think.   try to think think think.
try to think. think (like i said, into yr/own) think.
try to think. don't hurt yourself, i know it's new.
try to act,
act into thinking and think into action.
can u do it, hunh? i say hunh, can u stop moving like a drunk
gorilla?

                    ha ha   che che
                    ha ha   che che
                    ha ha   che che
                    ha ha   che che

move
what is u anyhow: a professional car watcher, a billboard for
nothingness, a sane madman, a reincarnated clark gable?
either you is or you ain't!

the deadliving
are the worldmakers,
the image breakers,
the rule takers: blackman can you stop a hurricane?

"I remember back in 1954 or '55, in Chicago, when we had
13 days without a murder, that was before them colored
people started calling themselves *black.*"
move.
move,
move to be moved,
move into yr/ownself, Clean.
Clean, u is the first black hippy i've ever met.
why u bes dressen so funny, anyhow, hunh?
i mean, is that u Clean?

why u bes dressen like an airplane, can u fly,
i mean,
will yr/blue jim-shoes fly u,
& what about yr/tailor made bell bottoms, Clean?
can they lift u above madness,
turn u into the right direction,
& that red & pink scarf around yr/neck what's that for Clean,
hunh?   will it help u fly, yeah, swing, swing   ing swing
            swinging high above telephone wires with dreams
            of this & that and illusions of trying to take bar-b-q
            ice cream away from lion minded niggers who
            didn't even know that *polish* is more than a
            sausage.
"clean as a tack,
rusty as a nail,
haven't had a bath
sence columbus sail."

when u goin be something real, Clean?
like yr/ own, yeah, when u goin be yr/ ownself?

the deadliving
are the worldmakers,
the image breakers,
the rule takers: blackman can u stop a hurricane, mississippi
            couldn't.
blackman if u can't stop what mississippi couldn't, *be it. be it.*
blackman be the wind, be the win, the win, the win, win win:

            wooooooooooowe boom boom   wooooooooooowe bah
            wooooooooooowe boom boom   wooooooooooowe bah
if u can't stop a hurricane, be one.
            wooooooooooowe boom boom   wooooooooooowe bah
            wooooooooooowe boom boom   wooooooooooowe bah
be the baddddest hurricane that ever came, a black hurricane.
            wooooooooooowe boom boom   wooooooooooowe bah
            wooooooooooowe boom boom   wooooooooooowe bah
the badddest black hurricane that ever came, a black
                        hurricane named Beulah,
go head Beulah, do the hurricane.
            wooooooooooowe boom boom   wooooooooooowe bah
            wooooooooooowe boom boom   wooooooooooowe bah

move
move to be moved from the un-moveable,
into our own, yr/self is own, yrself is own, own yourself.
go where you/we go, hear the unheard and do,
do the undone, do it, do it, do it *now,* Clean
and tomorrow your sons will
be alive to praise
you.

change-up,
let's go for ourselves
both cheeks are broken now.
change-up,
move past the corner bar,
let yr/spirit lift u above that quick high.
change-up,
that tooth pick you're sucking on was
once a log.
change-up,
and yr/children will look at u differently
than   we looked at our parents.

Dudley Randall

ROSES AND REVOLUTIONS

Musing on roses and revolutions,
I saw night close down on the earth like a great dark wing,
and the lighted cities were like tapers in the night,
and I heard the lamentations of a million hearts
regretting life and crying for the grave,
and I saw the Negro lying in the swamp with his face blown
   off,
and in northern cities with his manhood maligned and felt
   the writhing
of his viscera like that of the hare hunted down or the bear
   at bay,
and I saw men working and taking no joy in their work
and embracing the hard-eyed whore with joyless excite-
   ment
and lying with wives and virgins in impotence.

And as I groped in darkness
and felt the pain of millions,
gradually, like day driving night across the continent,
I saw dawn upon them like the sun a vision
of a time when all men walk proudly through the earth
and the bombs and missiles lie at the bottom of the ocean
like the bones of dinosaurs buried under the shale of eras,
and men strive with each other not for power or the ac-
   cumulation of paper
but in joy create for others the house, the poem, the game
   of athletic beauty.

Then washed in the brightness of this vision,
I saw how in its radiance would grow and be nourished and
   suddenly
burst into terrible and splendid bloom
the blood-red flower of revolution.

PRIMITIVES

Paintings with stiff
homuncules, flat in iron
draperies, with distorted
bodies against spaceless
landscapes.

Poems of old
poets in stiff
metres whose harsh
syllables
drag like
dogs with
crushed
backs.

We go back to
them, spurn difficult
grace and
symmetry,
paint tri-faced
monsters,
write lines that
do not sing, or
even croak, but that
bump,
jolt, and are hacked
off in the mid-
dle, as if by these dis-
tortions, this
magic, we can
exorcise
horror, which we
have seen and fear to
see again:

hate deified,
fears and
guilt conquering,
turning cities to
gas, powder and a
little rubble.

THE RITE

"Now you must die," the young one said,
"and all your art be overthrown."
The old one only bowed his head
as if those words had been his own.

And with no pity in his eyes
the young man acted out his part
and put him to the sacrifice
and drank his blood and ate his heart.

HAIL, DIONYSOS

Hail, Dionysos,
god of frenzy and release, of trance and visions,
hail to the manifestations of your might,
thanks for admitting me to your ritual.

Inspirer of divine speech:
        da da da da da da da da da;
releaser of subterranean energies:
        a man lies snoring on the sofa;
giver of fierce grace:
        a girl staggers among chairs, reels against the wall:
endower with new sensations and powers:
        a man vomits on the rug—an aromatic painting,
        and a girl, a lovely creature,
        wets her panties.

Hail Dionysos,
god of frenzy and release, of trance and visions.

I see them recede,
handsome men, beautiful women,
brains clever and bright, spirits gay and daring,
see eyes turn glassy, tongues grow thick,
limbs tremble and shake,
caught in your divine power,
carried away on the stream of your might,
Dionysos.

BALLAD OF BIRMINGHAM

"Mother dear, may I go downtown
instead of out to play,
and march the streets of Birmingham
in a freedom march today?"

"No, baby, no, you may not go,
for the dogs are fierce and wild,
and clubs and hoses, guns and jails
ain't good for a little child."

"But, mother, I won't be alone.
Other children will go with me,
and march the streets of Birmingham
to make our country free."

"No, baby, no, you may not go,
for I fear those guns will fire.
But you may go to church instead,
and sing in the children's choir."

She has combed and brushed her nightdark hair,
and bathed rose petal sweet,
and drawn white gloves on her small brown hands,
and white shoes on her feet.

The mother smiled to know her child
was in the sacred place,
but that smile was the last smile
to come upon her face.

For when she heard the explosion,
her eyes grew wet and wild.
She raced through the streets of Birmingham
calling for her child.

She clawed through bits of glass and brick,
then lifted out a shoe.
"O, here's the shoe my baby wore,
but, baby, where are you?"

THE SOUTHERN ROAD

There the black river, boundary to hell,
And here the iron bridge, the ancient car,
And grim conductor, who with surly yell
Forbids white soldiers where the black ones are.
And I re-live the enforced avatar
Of shuddering journey to a savage abode
Made by my sires before another war;
And I set forth upon the southern road.

To a land where shadowed songs like flowers swell
And where the earth is scarlet as a scar
Friezed by the bleeding lash that fell (O fell)
Upon my fathers' flesh. O far, far, far
And deep my blood has drenched it. None can bar
My birthright to the loveliness bestowed
Upon this country haughty as a star.
And I set forth upon the southern road.

This darkness and these mountains loom a spell
Of peak-roofed town where yearning steeples soar
And the holy holy chanting of a bell
Shakes human incense on the throbbing air
Where bonfires blaze and quivering bodies char.
Whose is the hair that crisped, and fiercely
      glowed?
I know it; and my entrails melt like tar
And I set forth upon the southern road.

O fertile hillsides where my fathers are,
From which my griefs like troubled streams have
      flowed,
I have to love you, though they sweep me far.
And I set forth upon the southern road.

GEORGE

When I was a boy desiring the title of man
And toiling to earn it
In the inferno of the foundry knockout,
I watched and admired you working by my side,
As, goggled, with mask on your mouth and shoulders
      bright with sweat,
You mastered the monstrous, lumpish cylinder blocks,
And when they clotted the line and plunged to the floor
With force enough to tear your foot in two,
You calmly stepped aside.

One day when the line broke down and the blocks
      reared up
Groaning, grinding, and mounted like an ocean wave
And then rushed thundering down like an avalanche,
And we frantically dodged, then braced our heads
      together
To form an arch to life and stack them,
You gave me your highest accolade:
You said: "You not afraid of sweat. You strong as a
      mule."

Now, here, in the hospital,
In a ward where old men wait to die,
You sit, and watch time go by.
You cannot read the books I bring, not even
Those that are only picture books,
As you sit among the senile wrecks,
The psychopaths, the incontinent.

One day when you fell from your chair and stared at
      the air
With the look of fright which sight of death inspires,
I lifted you like a cylinder block, and said,
"Don't be afraid
Of a little fall, for you'll be here
A long time yet, because you're strong as a mule."

BOOKER T. AND W.E.B.
(Booker T. Washington and W.E.B. Du Bois)

"It seems to me," said Booker T.,
"It shows a mighty lot of cheek
To study chemistry and Greek
When Mister Charlie needs a hand
To hoe the cotton on his land,
And when Miss Ann looks for a cook,
Why stick your nose inside a book?"

"I don't agree," said W.E.B.
"If I should have the drive to seek
Knowledge of chemistry or Greek,
I'll do it. Charles and Miss can look
Another place for hand or cook.
Some men rejoice in skill of hand,
And some in cultivating land,
But there are others who maintain
Their right to cultivate the brain."

"It seems to me," said Booker T.,
"That all you folks have missed the boat
Who shout about the right to vote,
And spend vain days and sleepless nights
In uproar over civil rights.
Just keep your mouths shut, do not grouse,
But work, and save, and buy a house."

"I don't agree," said W.E.B.,
"For what can property avail
If dignity and justice fail?
Unless you help to make the laws,
They'll steal your house with trumped-up clause.
A rope's as tight, a fire as hot,
No matter how much cash you've got.
Speak soft, and try your little plan,
But as for me, I'll be a man."

"It seems to me," said Booker T.—

"I don't agree,"
Said W.E.B.

THE PROFILE ON THE PILLOW

After our fierce loving
in the brief time we found to be together,
you lay in the half light
exhausted, rich,
with your face turned sideways on the pillow,
and I traced the exquisite
line of your profile, dark against the white,
delicate and lovely as a child's.

Perhaps
you will cease to love me,
or we may be consumed in the holocaust,
but I keep, against the ice and the fire,
the memory of your profile on the pillow.

James Randall

EXECUTION

It's just no use,
trying to be like them.
One comes, a giant
With filmy surgeon's gloves,
to put out your life. Click!
"The switches are going
to be shut down, one by one.
Your kinky hair. Click!
Your black face. Click!
Your nose, eyes, skin . . . Click!

In the anteroom, where
you've been waiting all your life,
the female of the species,
Carnivorous Destructi,
wheels by a steel cart piled with
human organs.
The rubber tires black the floor.
Electricity spills
from her blonde hair. The room
juggles, fades, reappears.
But it's no use, madam,
none of this will work.

That afternoon gloves returns,
to show you, to make you see, to plead.
There are large tears in his eyes.
Become, he says.
Join us. You are a dead race.
Nigger.

When? Perhaps never.
Perhaps it will never come,
falling down to wings,
a circling plummet to water.
Oh! the very last
beautiful, the body turning
and twisting in the maw of the sea.
Nigger.

"Come now, don't be
afraid, the doctor won't
the doctor won't
the doctor . . . "

In the cell your eyes
suck up the porridge of light.
The caucasian gods hover around you.
A Mechanism descends.
You are outside yourself.
Because it is no longer possible
to be yourself,
you become no one.
You know it is possible to be mad.
You carry your head under your arms.
The nurse spits on it.
The spittle bites:
Nigger!
Her butt is swaying under the white.

They take away the nothing that was yours.
Better to die, you think.
But nothing happens.

WHO SHALL DIE

Walk out into your country.
Whose is it?
Not the "polack's" not the "fascist's" or the "immigrant's,"
Or the "nigger's" with his dreams bitten off.
It belongs to no one,
Those who profess to love it
Feel nothing in the quagmire of broken faces
Where reprehensible magnates step,
The cry of the smallest bird is buried
In 200 years of filth shit on:
So the human being, defiled, chokes
On the wrongness of his dream,
Is gorged with chrome, steel, and vomits up
The excrement of slums.
He who shall die, buried to his eyes
In the racist hegemony, in the backward-running
Movie called the rights of man,
He who shall die unlamented, part of the nation still,
Whatever the politicians promise
In this or that election year . . . Nothing happens.

> By a white stream, in a white dream,
> A white God with white ideas,
> White as a white dove whom no one will love,
> The dove of death.

"Large commercial investments required . . ."
"The ghetto is a sociological phenomenon . . ."
"They're better off as they are . . ."
Nothing happens.
The aspirations of nation, ethic.
What are these?
There is a nightwind,
There is a blowing
There is a bloodletting of the mind.
To the universally dispossessed,
There is
The sterilization of desire. In these
Such a wind is building,
Harsh by night, in a darkness

With no silence,
Cricket-words buried.

Those who are hated shall surely
Give hate in return,
Those who are despised shall despise equally.
But all the poets of the world's past,
Pushed on by dreams and great deeds,
Cannot match the beauty of one
Who sits alone
In a house someone else owns,
Who very carefully,
Who very slowly
Pulls out a long blade,
Who slit his throat . . .

SEASCAPE

I think of surf coming quick
Along the granite piles, how the white
Foam holds no animal
Fang, and in breaking performs
A rhythm greater
Than the human heart.
It is what occurs
Singularly that matters—
A perception, always for the first time,
That the artist
Touches with honesty and love.

MY CHILDHOOD

In the church
of stained glass
the snow
against the colored window
the weight
of twelve stone eagles
overgrown with ice
the barbaric
splendor
the stone again
the draperies again
the candles again
the casket bundling
the little girl
in the church
that winter
in my childhood

Little sister who never lived,
I come home
at night
all burning
mourning
I don't know why,
to lay the cool muzzle
of my cheek
against your memory,
again the person
you could not be
without tears or joy or hurt
floods me with flowers

John Raven

ASSAILANT

He jumped me while I was asleep.
He was big and fat.
I been in many fights before,
but never one like that.
The only way I could survive,
was to get my hat . . .
His *name?*
Officer, I ain't talkin' 'bout no man;
I'm talkin' 'bout a rat!

REPTILE

Ole two-faced Nellie,
who likes to tattle,
moves about on her belly,
and has a rattle.

THE ROACH

A roach
came struttin
across my bedroom
floor,
like it was beyond
reproach,
or was
some sexy-lookin
whore,
and if I hadn't
snuffed it, had
left it
alive,
I know it would've
come right up
and gave me
five!

AN INCONVENIENCE

Mama,
papa,
and us
10 kids
lived in
a single room.
Once, when I
got sick
and like to die,
I heard a cry
slice through the gloom
"Hotdog!
We gon have
mo room!"

Sonia Sanchez

TO ALL BROTHERS

yeah.
        they
hang you up
those grey chicks
parading their
tight asses
in front of you.
some will say out
right
        baby i want
        to ball you
while smoother
ones will in
tegrate your
blackness
            yeah.
        brother
this sister knows
        and waits.

POEM AT THIRTY

it is midnight
no magical bewitching
hour for me
i know only that
i am here waiting
remembering that
once as a child
i walked two
miles in my sleep.
did i know
then where i
was going?
traveling. i'm
always traveling.

136

i want to tell
you about me
about nights on a
brown couch when
i wrapped my
bones in lint and
refused to move.
no one touches
me anymore.
father do not
send me out
among strangers.
you you black man
stretching scraping
the mold from your body.
here is my hand.
i am not afraid
of the night.

BLACK MAGIC

magic
        my man
is you
        turning
my body into
a thousand
smiles.
        black
magic is your
touch
        making
me breathe.

SUMMARY

no sleep tonight
not even after all
the red and green pills
i have pumped into
my stuttering self or
the sweet wine
that drowns them.

          this is
a poem for the world
for the slow suicides
in seclusion.
somewhere on 130th st.
a woman, frail as a
child's ghost, sings

          oh.
          oh. what
can the matter be? johnny's
so long at the fair.

          /i learned how
            to masturbate
thru the new york times.
i thought
shd i have
thought anything
that cd not
be proved. i
thought and
was wrong. listen.

             fool

     black
         bitch
of fantasy. life
is no more than

        gents
          and
            gigolos
            (99% american)
      liars
       and
      killers (199% american) dreamers

                    and drunks (299%
                                        american)
            (only god is 300% american)
                                    i say
        is everybody happy?
        this is a poem for me.
        i am alone.
        one night of words
        will not change
        all that.

A POEM FOR MY FATHER

        how sad it must be
        to love so many women
        to need so many black
        perfumed bodies weeping
        underneath you.
                            when i remember all those nights
        i filled my mind with
        long wars between short
        sighted trojans & greeks
        while you slapped some
        wide hips about in
        your pvt dungeon,
        when i remember your
        deformity   i want to
        do something about your
        makeshift manhood.
        i guess
                that is why
        on meeting your sixth
        wife, i cross myself
        with her confessionals.

A/NEEDED/POEM/ FOR MY SALVATION

am gonna take me seriously.
                    now.have

taken parents / schoooool / children / friends /
poets / seriously.
                    (have known
                              the cracker to be
SERIOUSLY DANGEROUS)
                              have taken day / time /
nite / time / rhetoric
                    seriously and been wounded
by / lovers of slick / blk / rappin
                              (in blker words:
pimps & jivers)
            am gonna loooook in a
mirror each time i pass one.
                              smile at my image
& say. yeh sistuh. it ain't easy.
                              but mooooove
beautifullee on passsst it.
                    keep on holden yo / head higher
cuz yo / bessssst is yet to
                    coooome.
am gonna take me seriously.
                    toooday.
& study myself.
                              git a phd in soniasanchezism.
& dare any motha / fucka
                    to be an authority on
me.
      (cuz i'll be wounded with sonia / learnen /
      beauty / love and will be dangerous)
                                        yeh. all
things considered.
                    gonna be serious bout
meeeeeee and livvvvve.

WE A badddDDD PEOPLE
(for gwendolyn brooks
a fo real bad one)

          i mean.
                    we bees real
          bad.
                we gots bad songs
          sung on every station
          we gots some bad   N A T U R A L S
          on our heads
                          and brothers gots
          some bad loud (fo real)
                dashiki threads
                            on them.
                                    i mean when
          we dance   u know we be doooen it

                                        when we talk
                                        we be doooen it

                        when we rap
                        we be doooen it
                                and
          when we love. well. yeh. u be knowen
          bout that too.   (uh-huh!)
                                    we got some BAADDD
          thots and actions
                            like off those white mothafuckers
                            and rip it off if it ain't nailed
                            down and surround those wite/
                            knee / grow / pigs & don't let them
                            live to come back again into
                            our neighborhoods (we ain't
                            no museum for wite
                            queer/minds/dicks/to
                                        fuck us up)
          and we be gitten into a
          SPIRITUAL thing.
                            like discipline
          of the mind.
          soul. body.   no drinken cept to celebrate
          our victories / births.

no smoken.   no shooten
needles into our blk / veins
         full of potential blk/
gold cuz our
     high must come from
     thinking working
     planning fighting loving
     our blk / selves
         into nationhood.
i mean.
     when we spread ourselves thin over our
     land and see our young / warriors /
     sistuhs moven / runnen on blk /
     hills of freedom.
        we'll boo ga loo
in love.
     aaa-ee-ooo-wah / wah
     aaa-ee-ooo-wah / wah
     aaa-ee-ooo-wah / wah
     aaa-ee-ooo-wah / wah

     git em with yo bad self. don. rat now.
     go on & do it. dudley. rat now. yeah.
     run it on down. gwen. rat now. yeah. yeah.

     aaa-e-oooooo. wah / wah.
     aaa-e-oooooo. wah / wah.
we a BAAAADDD people

        & we be gitting
        BAAAADDER
          every day.

LIFE / POEM

     shall i die
        shall i die
     a sweet / death
     a sweet / blk / death
        when the time
     comes, when it comes.

shall i scream
            shall i scream
a loud / scream
a long / loud / scream
                    of blk / ness over
chalk / colored   A MU RICA

shall i kill
            shall i kill
a quick / kill
a quick / spiritual / kill
                        full of remembered
past / blk / deaths /
                    murderings

and
shall i give the death cry
shall i give the death cry
                    ah - eh - eee - ooo - AH
                    ah - eh - eee - ooo - AH
i - eh - eee - ou - ahhh!
i - eh - eee - ou - ahhh!
                    aeae - oooo - um
                    aeae - oooo - um.
                            as i twirl/
move in to
            killing   hood.   for
my people.
            for my beautiful /
                        blk /
                            people.
shall i die   ——— now.
shall i die   ——— now.
                        a sweet / death
a sweet / blk / dance /
                    death
for the time is
coming   soon.
            for the time is
                        coming
                            soooooon.

SO THIS IS OUR REVOLUTION

nigguhs with naturrrals
still smoken pot drinken
shooten needles into they arms
for some yestuhday dreams.
sistuhs fucken other sistuh's
husbands
        cuz the rev o lu shun dun
freed them to fight the
enemy (they sistuhs)
                yeh.
                   the
revo lushun is here
            and we still
where our fathas /
            muthas were
twenty yrs ago
            cept we all look
prettier.
        cmon brothas.   sistuhs.
how bout a fo /
            real /   revolu/shun
with a fo / real
            battle to be fought
outside of bed /
            room / minds.
like. there are children
to be taught to love they blk/ selves
a blk/culture
            to be raised on this
wite / assed / universe.
                how bout a
fo / real
        sun inspired life
                while
these modern / day / missionary /
    moon / people
go to the moon
            where they belong.

LET US BEGIN THE REAL WORK
(for Elijah Muhammad who
has begun)

let us begin the real work.
                        now.
let us take back our children from
vista/
        workers.   ywca/s
                    sunday/schools.
boy/
        girl/scouts of wite/amurica.
let us begin the work of
centuries. untold.
                        let us teach our
children
            what is to be learnnnnned
bout themselves.
                        us.   let us
honestlee begin
                    nation/hood
builden.
            for our children.
                            with our
minds/hands/souls.
                    with our blk/visions
for blk/lives.
                let us begin
the begin/en work now.
                            while our
children still
                remember us & looooove.

A BALLAD FOR STIRLING STREET
(to be sung)

jest finished readen a book
    bout howard street
guess it had to be written
    bout howard street
now someone shud write one
    bout stirling street
show the beauty of blk / culture
    on stirling street
need to hear bout brothers
    TCB/en on stirling street
need to see sun / wrapped / sisters
    on that black street
need to see Imamu and Ameena
    walken blue / indigo / tall
need to hear the loud harambees
    strike gainst the wall

jest finished readen a book bout
    howard street
i've read a whole lot of books like
    howard street
if each one of us moved to a
    howard street
and worked like they do on
    stirling street
wudn't be no mo howard sts at all
all the howard sts wud fall - fall - fall
and won't that be good.
                yeh. yeh.
                and won't that be good.
                    yeh. yeh. yeh.

Stephany

MOVING DEEP

2

(Because I have wandered long through my own darkness
and heard the echo of my voice.)

The elusive quality of these moments more than tender
shared because of you
does not escape me totally.

I am not so easily undone.
You will find me singing even when you are not happening
to me, only more inside than out now.

You will continue in me every hour.

That you discipline my passion in the this and this
patiently denied
will only find reflection in my sighs.

Otherwise, I too long for the quiet happy thought
of the quiet growth of what was there at first
and will be.

For it will be.

6

You are instantly enfolded
in the arms
of every warmth,

I know you not
but for a smile
that belongs only to you

your aloneness
is
your own.

7

Who is not a stranger still
even after making love,
or the morning after?

The interlude of sleep again divides
it is clear again where one body
ends and the next begins,

Think to think at each encounter,
we will be strangers still
even after making love

and long conversation,
even after meals and showers
together

and years of touching.
It is not often that the core
of what I am is lost in longing

and is less often filled.
I understand my clinging
to the thought of you.

8

My love when this is past
and you have turned away
—or I

and we are no longer
as we are today
I will be more

having known your love
I will be more
and not alone.

19

Who collects the pain
screamed
into
the blue black sky

The sorrow of
the afternoon
is marked by more
than falling leaves,

is strained into
a tear,
thundering against
the rain.

Margaret Walker

PROPHETS FOR A NEW DAY

1.
As the Word came to prophets of old,
As the burning bush spoke to Moses,
And the fiery coals cleansed the lips of Isaiah;
As the wheeling cloud in the sky
Clothed the message of Ezekièl;
So the Word of fire burns today
On the lips of our prophets in an evil age—
Our sooth-sayers and doom-tellers and doers of the Word.
So the Word of the Lord stirs again
These passionate people toward deliverance.
As Amos, Shepherd of Tekoa, spoke
To the captive children of Judah,
Preaching to the dispossessed and the poor,
So today in the pulpits and the jails,
On the highways and in the byways,
A fearless shepherd speaks at last
To his suffering weary sheep.

2.
So, kneeling by the river bank
Comes the vision to a valley of believers
So in flaming flags of stars in the sky
And in the breaking dawn of a blinding sun
The lamp of truth is lighted in the Temple
And the oil of devotion is burning at midnight
So the glittering censer in the Temple
Trembles in the presence of the priests
And the pillars of the door-posts move
And the incense rises in smoke
And the dark faces of the sufferers
Gleam in the new morning
The complaining faces glow
And the winds of freedom begin to blow
While the Word descends on the waiting World below.

3.
A beast is among us.
His mark is on the land.
His horns and his hands and his lips are gory with our blood.
He is War and Famine and Pestilence
He is Death and Destruction and Trouble
And he walks in our houses at noonday
And devours our defenders at midnight.
He is the demon who drives us with whips of fear
And in his cowardice
He cries out against liberty
He cries out against humanity
Against all dignity of green valleys and high hills
Against clean winds blowing through our living;
Against the broken bodies of our brothers.
He has crushed them with a stone.
He drinks our tears for water
And he drinks our blood for wine;
He eats our flesh like a ravenous lion
And he drives us out of the city
To be stabbed on a lonely hill.

JACKSON, MISSISSIPPI

City of tense and stricken faces
City of closed doors and ketchup splattered floors,
City of barbed wire stockades,
And ranting voices of demagogues,
City of squealers and profane voices;
Hauling my people in garbage trucks,
Fenced in by new white police billies,
Fist cuffs and red-necked brothers of Hate Legions
Straining their leashed and fiercely hungry dogs;
City of tree-lined, wide, white avenues
And black alleys of filthy rendezvous;
City of flowers: of new red zinnias
And oriental poppies and double-ruffled petunias
Ranch styled houses encircled with rose geranium
And scarlet salvia
And trouble-ridden minds of the guilty and the conscienceless;

City of stooges and flunkeys, pimps and prostitutes,
Bar-flies and railroad-station freaks;
City with southern sun beating down raw fire
On heads of blaring jukes,
And light-drenched streets puddled with the promise
Of a brand-new tomorrow
I give you my heart, Southern City
For you are my blood and dust of my flesh,
You are the harbor of my ship of hope,
The dead-end street of my life,
And the long washed down drain of my youth's years of toil,
In the bosom of your families
I have planted my seeds of dreams and visions and prophecies
All my fantasies of freedom and of pride,
Here lie three centuries of my eyes and my brains and my hands,
Of my lips and strident demands,
The graves of my dead,
And the birthing stools of grannies long since fled.
Here are echoes of my laughing children
And hungry minds of pupils to be fed.
I give you my brimming heart, Southern City.
For my eyes are full and no tears cry
And my throat is dusty and dry.

FOR ANDY GOODMAN— MICHAEL SCHWERNER— AND JAMES CHANEY

(Three Civil Rights Workers Murdered in Mississippi on June 21, 1964)
(Written After Seeing the Movie, *Andy In A.M.*)

Three faces . . .
    mirrored in the muddy stream of living . . .
young and tender like
quiet beauty of still water,
sensitive as the mimosa leaf,
    intense as the stalking cougar
    and impassive as the face of rivers;
The sensitive face of Andy
The intense face of Michael
The impassive face of Chaney.

Three leaves . . .
    Floating in the melted snow
    Flooding the Spring
    oak leaves
    one by one
    moving like a barge
    across the seasons
    moving like a breeze across the window pane
    winter . . . summer . . . spring
When is the evil year of the cricket?
When comes the violent day of the stone?
In which month
do the dead ones appear at the cistern?

Three lives . . .
    turning on the axis of our time
    Black and white together
    turning on the wheeling compass
    of a decade and a day
    The concerns of a century of time
    . . . an hourglass of destiny

Three lives . . .
    ripe for immortality of daisies and wheat
    for the simple beauty of a humming bird
    and dignity of a sequoia
    of renunciation and
    resurrection
For the Easter morning of our Meridians.

Why should another die for me?
Why should there be a calvary
A subterranean hell for three?
In miry clay?
In the muddy stream?
In the red misery?
In mutilating hatred and in fear?
The brutish and the brazen
without brain
without blessing
without beauty . . .
They have killed these three.
They have killed them for me.

Sunrise and sunset . . .
Spring rain and winter window pane . . .
I see the first leaves budding
The green Spring returning
I mark the falling
of golden Autumn leaves
and three lives floating down the quiet stream
Till they come to the surging falls . . .

The burned blossoms of the dogwood tree
tremble in the Mississippi morning
The wild call of the cardinal bird
troubles the Mississippi morning
I hear the morning singing
larks, robins, and the mocking bird
while the mourning dove
broods over the meadow
Summer leaf falls never turning brown
Deep in a Mississippi thicket
I hear that mourning dove
Bird of death singing in the swamp
Leaves of death floating in their watery grave

Three faces turn their ears and eyes
sensitive
intense
impassive
to see the solemn sky of summer
to hear the brooding cry
of the mourning dove

Mississippi bird of sorrow
O mourning bird of death
Sing their sorrow
Mourn their pain
And teach us death,
To love and live with them again!

Marvin X

PROVERBS

Blame not the world for your troubles, blame yourself.

Yes, I believe in peace. And there will be peace —— after the fight!

A fool was in heaven but didn't know it.

Allah will give you everything you need —— just be ready when it comes.

The first duty of a revolutionary is to clean his house.

Poets should study their poems.

TILL THE SUN GOES DOWN

Malika
What is this
That burns within me
Like a thousand suns
That stirs my being
To joyful madness
What have you done to me
No more than I have allowed you
Because of your Blackness
More precious to me
Then all the gold in Ghana
Than all the diamonds in Azania
Move me
Malika
Move me
And I will move mountains
Destroy cities
To be free with you
To be at peace with you
Till the sun goes down.

From
Black Poetry

Samuel Allen

VIEW FROM THE CORNER

Now the thing the Negro has GOT to do—
    I looked from my uncle to my dad
Yes, Nimrod, but the trouble with the NEGRO is—
    I looked from my dad to my uncle
I know, Joseph, but the FIRST thing the Negro's got to do—
    It was confusing . . .

This fellow, the Negro, I thought excitedly,
    must be in a very bad fix—
We'd all have to jump in and help
    —such trouble
    —all these things to do
I'd never HEARD of anybody with so many things to do
    —GOT to do!
I intensely disliked such things
    —go to school, wash your ears, wipe the dishes
And what the NEGRO had to do sounded worse than that!
He was certainly in a fix, this Negro, whoever he was.

    I was much concerned as I looked at my uncle
Now the thing the Negro has GOT to do—!

Ebon

**TO OUR FIRST BORN
OR THE PROPHET ARRIVES**
"minnie lou had a boychild this morning!"

> the night——
> blackbright with shadows that caress
> black breasts sagging with night fluid.
> breast-touching belly distended with
> bantubabyhood . . .
> a soulchild with mindheart
> to touch the quick nerve.
>
> a manchild whose roots
> extend beneath parosol shade trees
> with strange fruit above.
> bulge-eyed fruit screaming deeds
> to touch the quick nerve.
>
> a blackchild whose memories disrupt
> the waking sleep of blackpeople
> dreamwalking beneath a black sun.
> rooted memories
> to stir the quick deed!
>
> a godchild whose heart still sings
> this disquieting thing——
> a terrifying and strange gift!
> blackgift forcing child to be man
> and man to be god.
> a godchild with blackgifts
> to stir the quick deed!
>
> the night . . .
> blackbright with joy
> "minnie lou had *OUR* boychild this morning!"

September 1967

Etheridge Knight

FOR BLACK POETS
WHO THINK OF SUICIDE

Black Poets should live—not leap
From steel bridges (like the white boys do.
Black Poets should live—not lay
Their necks on railroad tracks (like the white boys do.
Black Poets should seek—but not search too much
In sweet dark caves, nor hunt for snipes
Down psychic trails (like the white boys do.

For Black Poets belong to Black People. Are
The Flutes of Black Lovers. Are
The Organs of Black Sorrows. Are
The Trumpets of Black Warriors.
Let all Black Poets die as trumpets,
And be buried in the dust of marching feet.

Doughtry Long

ONE TIME HENRY
DREAMED THE NUMBER

one time henry dreamed the number
but we didn't play it,
and do you know, that thing came out straight
3-67?
        yes it did!
we was both sick
for a whole week,
            could'a sure used
                        the money then too.
that was back in hoover's time
when folks was scufflin
to make ends meet.
i knock on wood though
                    we've lived through it all.
last night after we ate

the last of the meat loaf and greens
and was watching television
henry asked me if i rememberded that,
i told him yes,
                we laughed
                            then went to bed
and kept each other warm.

Edward S. Spriggs

FOR THE TRUTH
(because it is necessary)

in the tea rooms
of our revolution
we blatantly debate
our knowledge of world revolts
—our anxious ears only half-listened
to the songs of the martinique
who sings in muffled tones
from beneath a mechanized tombstone
built by the pulp of greedy merchants
who got stoned on the juices of our servitude
& who write prefaces to our "negritude"

from the tea rooms
of our revolution we emerge
to pamphleteer
the anticipatory designs
of our dead
& exiled poets
—without sanctions
from our unsuspecting brothers
whose death we so naively plot
(we engage in a hypothetical revolt
against a not-so-hypothetical enemy

what kind of man are you
black revolutionary, so-called?
what kind of man are you trying to be
ultra-hip-revolutionary-nationalist-

quasi-strategist-ego-centric-phony
intellectual romantic black prima donna child
—screaming "revolution means change . . . "
never finishing the sentence
or the thought
talking about "para-military"
strategy and techniques
publicizing a so-called underground program
wearing your military garb
as if you never heard of camouflage
so in love with intrigue
you have no thoughts
about the post-revolution life
that the total destruction
you talk about assumes . . .

you leave me quite confused
brother
i don't know who the enemy is
anymore
perhaps it is me, myself, because
i have these thoughts
in the tea rooms of our revolution.

From
Broadside Series

MARTIN LUTHER KING, JR.
GWENDOLYN BROOKS

A man went forth with gifts.

He was a prose poem.

He was a tragic grace.

He was a warm music.

He tried to heal the vivid volcanoes.

His ashes are
   reading the world.

His Dream still wishes to anoint
   the barricades of faith and of control.

His word still burns the center of the sun,
   above the thousands and the
   hundred thousands.

The word was Justice. It was spoken.

So it shall be spoken.

So it shall be done.

Gwendolyn Brooks, poet laureate of Illinois and a winner of the Pulitzer Prize, wrote this eulogy of the Rev. Dr. Martin Luther King, Jr. for *The Chicago Daily News*. It was printed April 5, 1968, the day after Dr. King's assassination.

A CHILD'S NIGHTMARE
By Bobb Hamilton

Oh what sound is that, what sound is that
Rolling from the valley yon?
Outshouting the sea and shaming the lion
It roars like the hounds of Zion,
It roars like the hounds of Zion.
> Child, it's just the wind you hear
> A-humming in the palms;
> It's just the wind you hear my child
> A-humming in the palms.

Oh what beast is that, is that, is that
Coming through the valley yon,
And breathing blackfire through teeth of brass?
Don't you hear its feet in the grass?
Don't you hear its feet in the grass?
> Hush, it's just the husbandmen
> Off to their vines this morn;
> It's just the early husbandmen
> Off to their vines this morn.

Oh what man is that, what man is that
Stumbling through the valley yon?
He's wearing a tree and a sack-cloth gown,
Look! He wears a spiked crown!
Look! He wears a spiked crown!
> It's just a man gone mad, my dove,
> Two thieves are there behind.
> It's just a man gone mad, my dove,
> Two thieves are there behind.

Oh how softly, sweetly glows his brow . . .
Look . . . he stumbled there and fell . . .
Would madness make us too so mild, so mild?
When he passed me by, he smiled,
When he passed me by, he smiled.
> That's no smile upon his face,
> It's a frown of agony;
> No smile is that upon his face,
> It's a frown of agony.

And now he's up on yonder hill,
And a crowd is there with him too,
Hark the thock, thock, on mallet, wood and nail.
. . . Oh, they've hoisted him up like a sail,
Oohh . . . look, he's hoisted up like a sail!

Sunny

(From an Old Photograph)

By Naomi Long Madgett

I wore a baseball cap, so like my brothers
I always tried to be. I climbed the trees,
Straddled the fences, daily skinned the knees
My brothers did. Gangly as all the others,
I played fair tackle, handled second base
With skill, and my left hook was pretty good.
But still, lone girl in all the neighborhood,
What could I do to run an equal race
With them? Despised for tender look and curl
Of hair, when games were ended, I was sneered
At, taunted and escaped from, mocked and jeered
Being still Daddy's Little Sunshine Girl.

What curse! The most unpardonable name
In any childhood scheme. What mute despair
His innocence subjected me to bear!
And yet, sometimes what magic with the shame!
Bunches of grapes I gained by being Me,
Kisses I was embarrassed to receive,
Stories of somewhere-lands I could believe
Heard in the place of honor at his knee,
And summer-long the shirtsleeve game of tag
All through the house and up and down the street,
The victory always mine, the trophy, sweet
Surprises hidden in a paper bag.

Oh, how I dream! What gentle winter gold
Fine-spun upon an old man's head I bless
And touch with unaccustomed tenderness
(Knowing myself at last) as I behold
How few there are who need no proof of worth
To find you still the sunshine of their earth.

Letter from a Wife

I retrace your path in my bare feet

Press my lips against your empty cup

Touch your clothes for now-gone warmth

View each object which your eyes beheld

Write your name and speak the same

I bless each day you elude the pack

Rehearse each word of love we spoke

Recall the vows your eyes declared

Your last touch lingers with me still

I face each day with dragging feet—weary heart

Apart-from-you takes half my strength

The rest I need for waiting.

S. Carolyn Reese

RACE RESULTS, U.S.A., 1966:

White Right—A Favorite—Wins;
Lurline—A Long Shot—Places;
Black Power—A Long Shot—Shows.

For Stokely Carmichael

BY SARAH WEBSTER FABIO

Blistering,
the lone black jockey's
ear deafens beneath
the roar of torments
hurled from Birmingham
bleachers by the helmeted
keepers of the leashed
law as their white hot
screams dare him dare
run the race; those
killers of his dreams
invade the bugle's blare,
spooking his steed; yet,
he's off!

Galloping,
furiously, the horses round
the curves and come into
the homestretch: in the
lead, it's White Right;
Lurline, in line for second;
and, wait, the black jockey,
eyeing the hateful hurdles
blocking him, grips tight
his reins for a quickening
thrust:

noses forward,
testily, heads out from
the dusty herd, and jeers
back at those who mourn
the lost purses of their
thoroughbreds. He spurs
on the dark horse to
the finish, toward his
fully reckoned, time-honed
hour of triumph.

Earth

FOR MRS. MARY BETHUNE AND THE
AFRICAN AND AFRO-AMERICAN WOMEN

By Askia Muhammad Toure'

Where are the warriors, the young men?
Who guards the women's quarters — the burnthaired
women's   quarters —
and hears their broken sobbing in the night?

To endure: to remain, like the red earth, strong
    and   fecundant.
Your coppery, chocolate, ebony warm-skin scoured
    . . . and   toughened
        by the arid wind.
The wrinkles in your eyes, your smiles, your
    frowning foreheads
are the Stars within your Crowns, my women.
Cares come and go; dreams fade away; sons are lost
on lonely battlefields . . . severed by the Nordic Meataxe.
Men are broken . . . babble . . . lift their bloody genitals
upon the tainted altar of the Snow Queen.
Her frigid, sterile smile is a tribute to the vengeance
    of her Caesars.
Where, then, is Spartacus, is Attila, is Hannibal?
Who thunders, now, upon those Seven Hills?
They are gone . . . and . . . *only you remain!*
You whose Womb has warmed the European hills and made
        the Pale Snows tawny.
Pagan Spain, sunny France, Italy and the fabled Grecian Isles
are drenched by the Sunlight of your smile.

> Mother of the World!
>
> Fecundant, Beating Heart!
>
> Enduring Earth!:
>
> *Only you remain!*

Where are the warriors, the young men?
Who guards the women's quarters? . . . . .

GHETTO WAIF

By B. FELTON

He strolled from door to door.
Merriment was galore.
In spirit he was rich.
Down the narrow streets he walked.
A man was sitting on a box, munching a piece of chicken,
As children ran and played.
Playing a child's favorite game, Last Night.
"Last night, night before, twenty-four robbers at my door.
I got up, let them in, hit them in the head with a rolling pin.
All hid?"
Down the street in front of a dilapidated building
Another game was going on . . .
"No laughing, no talking, no moving, red light. No moving, green
     light.
Don't move, Girl. You moved your arm. Come back," he said.
The little girl stuck out her tongue, at the same time switching her
Fat rump . . .
It was twilight . . .
The neon signs were on . . .
From a distance came the sound of voices singing.
Nearing the source of music, sighs, moans.
Shouts of "Hallelujah, Jesus."
"Save him Lord!"
"Well, it's all right," said the minister.
Standing back looking up at the roughly hand painted letters:
The Right Way Church of Holiness of the Apostolic Faith,
Bishop Hope, Founder and Pastor.
"Amen, amen, well, child, I know I've been born again.
I feel, I feel all right."
A boy on a bike whisked by with a bottle of beer.
Upstairs over the storefront church came the cry of a baby's
     voice.
A few doors down a record player was going full blast.
Children were doing the shimmy, the Chinese slop and the Wa-
     tusi.
A boy of about nine called out to his dancing partner.
"Work out, baby, shake that thing.
Let's get into something."
Next to Meatball's Inn were two cats talking about some broads.
"Man, I've got a broad, a dollar down and a dollar a week."
"You don't say," replied his friend.
"Man! That's the kind of broad I'm looking for.
Lay on, my man, lay on."
Smiling, then shaking his head,
He began to skip, down, down, down.
All the way down to forty-first street to Big Eva's
With a dime in his pocket he went inside and asked for a bottle of
Strawberry soda water and a straw.
Closing the door and sipping on the straw.
The cloak of night and the midnight sun lit his way along the
Lively streets.

black and white

By UMAR ABD RAHIM HASSON
(Tony Rutherford)

white america,
comfortable and disillusioned,
gave birth to a
black
beast that dwells
in the shadows and squalor of another world,

called nigger—lives
in the recesses of the
mind.

"niggerwoman comely (and
promiscuous!) i love you!
niggerman
sought by miss ann
i envy you!
black negotiators kneeling
at my white altar
i need you!
protect me!"

whiteys lie there,
sun warming and loving them,
alms to the cause
are given while
they smother
a black mother
pregnant with dignity.

where is a handsome and strong
bitter and struggling Power to save—
to tell black mother
that the evening sun also loves her?

a black man in the shadows shouts
and the Power is therein.

174

THE SQUARED CIRCLE

By CARL KILLEBREW

This is the way
it goes,
I hate to fight a
          brother.
          My trainer says
          this is my route
               take it slow.
          after round one
          it's plain to see
          his style is made
                    for me.

My left, it's as quick
          as my stiletto,
          the right is
          my bomb, when
          I tag
          him
          he goes numb.
          I'm sorry,
          brother
          but you're
          my ticket
          out
          of this ghetto.

OUR DAYS
ARE NUMBERED

By ALICIA L. JOHNSON

what can i say
when she says/
i'm glad you're
doing something constructive.

like shooting stars
our days are numbered

i want to
TEAR ROOFS
with my poems
BREAK BACKS
with brittled lines
and cause
WALLS TO CRUMBLE
at each
constant stanza.

what can i say
when she says/
i'm glad you're
doing something constructive.

MY days
are numbered brother
POETS days
are numbered too
it is for U
that i write
it will help Y-O-U
when ROOFS TEAR
BACKS BREAK
AND
WALLS CRUMBLE
IN
STANZAS.

To Dudley

In

Peace !

Alicia Johnson
4-7-69

T.C.

(Terry Callier; True Christian)

BY WALTER BRADFORD

And the voices dropped
                        from the ashy ceiling like pellets of rain
foreshadowing his coming;
                        "A Gemini's Sun" they cried, "born to trudge
between the parallels of the heavenly twins."
        And he does that with a guitar for a crucifix and six thin
palms for strings (all of them mean actors)
                                while strolling down the dan
ry-an eXpressway, with a forty pound VOO DOO radiator on his back
        and
a red ban-dan-na tied around his head singing, "I have seen all the
light!"
        While some stillborn monkey niggahs
                                with steel knuckles for asses
in chartreuse pants and fishtail shoes, swing ape-style on the 51st
street overpass screaming: "Moses, is you back again?"
        And they streamed on behind him till the concreteness
                stopped at
the base of MECCA'S hill
                        just to hear
                        TERRY CALLIER SING!
        And young 63rd street pharaohs cloaked in Blackstone's label
                gave
peace hosannas to Disciples, for
                        creation was order, it was peace.
        So instead of some bible-fiction god rebuilding this world let
Nommo-child Terry Callier sing the first seven days.
        True christian, please make your world.

GRANNY BLAK POET
(in Pastel)

By ARTHUR PFISTER

                    some people say
                    she's . . . . . hung up
                    in
                        pastels/ lacy poems/ lacy scarves/ lacy
                        afro
                            ʌwigs/ lacy dresses
(and some other things
  i won't mention
  or her oldman might
     get on my case)
                        but
                            u/ we (*BLAK* people)
                                            . . . can see the truth
                        about her
                                "hangup"
                                    . . . *BLAK* ness
                                            (can u dig?
                                        not *graves*
                                i mean
            like slaves
                    &chains
                        &irony lace
                            &other
                                    . . . things
    i mean
        i *thought*
                she was a jiver
                        —talked about her grandson
                        (every third word)

for Mrs. Margaret Danner

i mean
      i *thought*
             she was a jiver
                        —afro down
                                 and all
          but
            then
            Granny *BLAK* poet
            —*poeted*—
                    and u/we(*BLAK*people)
                          . . . could see the truth
hip thang to see Granny *BLAK* poet
whirling
      poems,counterpoems
sweet thang to see Granny *BLAK* poet
whirling
      boogaloowords
mean thang to see Granny *BLAK* poet
whirling
      thru irony lace,&miles &miles
               &tongues &tongues
               of grandsons . . .
      BLAK thang to see Granny *BLAK* poet
                 whirling
                     whirling
               sweet,soft songs
               that stir
               the hearts of women . . .
                 & the *blood*
                    of warriors . . .

NOW AIN'T THAT LOVE?

By Carolyn M. Rodgers

who would
who could
    understand that
when i'm near him
i am a skinny, dumb, knock-kneed
lackey, drooling on the words of
my maharajah (or what/ever they call them
                    in those jive textbooks)

me. i am a bitch. hot.
panting for a pat from his hand
so i can wag my
love in front of his
    face. a princess, black.
dopey with lust, waiting
for the kiss of action from my
    prince. I know that this
whole scene is not
    cool, but it's real!
so a-live--- dig it! sometimes, we be so close
    i can cop his pulse
and think it's my heart that i
    hear
in my ears. uh. now ain't that love?

RIP-OFF

By Ronda M. Davis

naw
naw, little brotha,
u don't shoot no – brotha!
don't care WHAT
he said/u said/NOBODY said
he done   done.

brotha never ripped-u-off
a con-ti-nent.
brotha wouldn't think to
snatch yo youth/
tear up yo mind/
wring out yo spirit
before u knew u
had one.

brotha wouldn't want to
slash yo tongue
so u couldn't open/close yo mouth
talk no talk
rap no rap
cause it hurts   yo image   to be yoself.

dig it. it wudn't brotha
who made yo iiizzze SO HARD!

naw
naw, little brotha,
brotha straight.
he broke/broken like u
tighten up   maaan
u don't chop down no
brotha

u just call him a mothafucka
and move on.

Author Index

Title Index

BROADSIDE SERIES—SINGLE POEMS

Portfolio of Broadsides .... $ .50
1. Ballad of Birmingham, by Dudley Randall .... .50
2. Dressed All in Pink, by Dudley Randall .... .50
3. Gabriel, by Robert Hayden .... .50
4. Ballad of the Free, by Margaret Walker .... .50
5. The Sea Turtle and The Shark, by M. B. Tolson .... .50
6. We Real Cool, by Gwendolyn Brooks .... .50
7. A Poem for Black Hearts, by LeRoi Jones .... .50
8. Booker T. and W. E. B., by Dudley Randall .... .50
9. A Child's Nightmare, by Bobb Hamilton .... .50
11. Sunny, by Naomi Long Madgett .... .50
12. Letter from a Wife, by Carolyn Reese .... .50
13. Backlash Blues, by Langston Hughes .... .50
14. Race Results, U.S.A., 1966, by Sarah W. Fabio .... .50
15. Song of The Son, by Jean Toomer .... .50
16. Back Again, Home, by Don L. Lee .... .50
17. The Black Narrator, by Le Graham .... .50
18. Black Madonna, by Harold Lawrence .... .50
19. The Wall, by Gwendolyn Brooks .... .50
20. At That Moment, by Raymond Patterson .... .50
21. 2 Poems for Black Relocation Centers, by Etheridge Knight .... .50
22. Not Light, Nor Bright, Nor Feathery, by Margaret Danner .... .50
23. At Bay, by James A. Emanuel .... .50
24. Earth, by Askia Muhammad Toure' .... .50
27. Ghetto Waif, by B. Felton .... .50
28. Black and White, by Tony Rutherford .... .50
31. T.C. (Terry Callier, True Christian), by Walter Bradford .... .50
32. Ginger Bread Mama, by Doughtry Long .... .50
33. One Sided Shoot-Out, by Don L. Lee .... .50
35. Granny Blak Poet (in pastel), by Arthur Pfister .... .50
36. For Black Poets Who Think of Suicide, by Etheridge Knight .... .50
37. Now Ain't That Love?, by Carolyn Rodgers .... .50
38. Slaughterhouse, by Helen Pulliam .... .50
39. County Jail, by Jill Witherspoon .... .50
40. Rip-Off, by Ronda Davis .... .50
41. All I Gotta Do, by Nikki Giovanni .... .50
42. Goodnight, by Paula Alexander .... .50
43. Muslim Men, by Sterling Plumpp .... .50
44. Long Rap/Commonly Known as a Poetic Essay, by Carolyn Rodgers ..... .50
45. The Nigger Cycle, by Kuweka Amiri Mwandishe .... .50
46. A Simple Poem To Mae, by Omari Kenyetta Tarajia (R. C. James III) .... .50
47. Black Henry, by Rockie Taylor (Tejumola Ologboni) .... .50
48. Two Poems, by Robert Keeby and Stephany .... .50
49. Tears and Kisses, by James Amaker, Glenda Gracia, Porter Kirkwood, Lori Lunford,
      and Wilbert Rutledge, Jr. .... .50
50. For H. W. Fuller, by Carolyn M. Rodgers .... .50
51. Poems, by Bobb Hamilton, George Buggs .... .50
52. Poems, by Yusuf, Jeanne Newkirk Smith, Robert T. Bowen, Carole Gregory Clemmons .... .50
53. Poems, by Hodari Kinamo, LaDonna Tolbert, B. H. Rogers, Alvin Kingcade .... .50
54. Poems, by Lawrence C. Riley, Thomas Washington, Jr., Robert L. Mabarut Khalilmalik .... .50

BROADSIDE VOICES

Broadside Album: Rappin' and Readin', by Don L. Lee $5.00
Broadside on Broadway: Seven Poets Read (cassette) 5.00
Tapes of poets reading their own books (reels and cassettes) 5.00
   Tapes by Emanuel, Giovanni, Jeffers, Hodges, Knight, Randall, Arnez & Murphy, Sanchez, Eckels,
Marvin X, Stephany Lee, Kgositsile, Walker, Danner, Brooks.

BROADSIDE POSTERS

1. For Black Poets Who Think of Suicide, by Etheridge Knight $1.50
2. On Getting a Natural, by Dudley Randall 1.00
3. Black Silhouette, by Pat Whitsitt 1.00
4. Angela, by Talita Long 1.00
5. Protect the Sister, by Reginald Payne & Pearl Eckles 2.00

THE BLACK POSITION—A PERIODICAL (Annual) $1.00

BROADSIDE POETS

Against the Blues, by Alvin Aubert. 0-910296-73-1 .... paper $1.50

Aloneness (children's), by Gwendolyn Brooks. .... Cloth 0-910296-75-8 $3.00 paper 0-910296-55-3 1.00

Beer Cans, Bullets, Things & Pieces, by Arthur Pfister. 0-910296--29-4 .... 1.25

Black Arts: An Anthology of Black Creations, Edited by Ahmed Alhamisi and Harun Kofi Wangara. (Black Arts Publications) 910296-06-5 .... 3.50

Black Feeling, Black Talk, by Nikki Giovanni. 910296-31-6 .... 1.00

Black Judgement, by Nikki Giovanni. 910296-07-3 .... 1.00

Black Love Black Hope, by Doughtry Long. 0-910296-20-0 .... 1.00

Black Man Listen, by Marvin X. 910296-08-1 .... tape $5.00, book 1.00
  Poems and Proverbs voice the philosophy of the Nation of Islam.

Black Poetry: A Supplement to Anthologies Which Exclude Black Poets, Edited by Dudley Randall. 910296-09-X .... cloth $4.00, paper .95

Black Pride, by Don L. Lee. 910296-04-9 .... 1.00
  The second book by the impressive young Chicago poet.

Black Velvet, by Everett Hoagland. 910296-34-0 .... 1.00

Black Wisdom, by Frenchy Jolene Hodges. 0-910296-40-5 .... tape $5.00, paper 1.00

Blues For Mama, by John Raven. 0-910296-54-5 .... .50

The Broadside Annual, 1972, ed. Jill Witherspoon. 0-910296-77-4 .... Paper 1.00

A Broadside Treasury, 1965-1970, Edited by Gwendolyn Brooks.
  cloth 0-910296-53-7 $6.00, paper 0-910296-51-0 4.00

Cities Burning, by Dudley Randall. 910296-10-3 .... tape $5.00, book 1.00
  Reflects the troubled emotions and tragic events of our time.

Directionscore: Selected and New Poems, by Don L. Lee.
  paper ISBN 0-910296-48-8 $3.75, cloth 0-910296-49-0 $6.00 Special Edition 0-910296-50-2 15.00

Don't Ask Me Who I Am, by James Randall, Jr. 910296-46-4 .... 1.00

Don't Cry, Scream, by Don L. Lee. 910296-11-1 .... tape $5.00, cloth $4.50, paper 1.50
  A brilliant, devastating book by a leading young poet.

Down Nigger Paved Streets, by William A. Thigpen, Jr. 0-910296-74-X .... paper 1.00

Dynamite Voices: Black Poets of the 1960's, by Don L. Lee. ISBN 0-910296-33-2 .... 2.75

Family Pictures, by Gwendolyn Brooks. 910296-43-X .... tape $5.00, cloth $5.00, paper 1.00

For Malcolm: Poems on the Life and the Death of Malcolm X, Edited by Dudley Randall and Margaret Burroughs. 910296-12-X .... cloth $4.95, paper 2.95

Frank, by Carolyn Thompson (a children's book). 910296-41-3 .... 1.00

Guerilla Warfare, by Ahmed Alhamisi. (Black Arts Publications) 1.00

Home Is Where the Soul Is, by Jon Eckels. 910296-00-6 .... tape $5.00, book 1.00
  A young California poet who is together and relevant.

Homecoming, by Sonia Sanchez. 910296-05-7 .... tape $5.00, book 1.00
  A passionate, earthy first book by a gifted poet.

Impressions of African Art, by Margaret Danner. 910296-13-8 .... 1.00

It's A New Day (a children's book), by Sonia Sanchez. 0-910296-60-X ...... Cloth $4.00, paperback 1.25

Jump Bad: a New Chicago Anthology, Edited by Gwendolyn Brooks. 0-910296-32-2 .... paper 4.00

Life Styles, by Marion Alexander Nicholes. ISBN 0-910296-36-7 .... 1.00

More to Remember: Poems of Four Decades, by Dudley Randall. (Third World Press)
  cloth 0-910296-59-6 $5.00, paper 0-910296-58-8 1.95

Moving Deep, by Stephany. 910296-18-9 .... tape $5.00, book 1.00
  Love poems by a young new poet and artist.

My Blackness Is the Beauty of This Land, by Lance Jeffers. 910296-28-6 .... tape $5.00, paper 1.00

Our Business in the Streets, by Jon Eckels. ISBN 0-910296-31-6 .... paper 1.00

Panther Man, by James A. Emanuel. 910296-35-9 .... tape $5.00, paper 1.00

Poem Counterpoem, by Margaret Danner and Dudley Randall. 910296-14-6 .... tape $5.00, book 1.00
  A unique arrangement of paired poems by two poets of longstanding distinction.

Poems From Prison, by Etheridge Knight. 910296-15-4 .... tape $5.00, paper 1.00

Prophets for a New Day, by Margaret Walker. 910296-21-9 .... tape $5.00, paper 1.00

Re:Creation, by Nikki Giovanni. 910296-47-2 .... tape $5.00, cloth $4.50, paper 1.50

Riot, by Gwendolyn Brooks. 910296-19-7 .... cloth $5.00, paper 1.00
  A long poem by the Pulitzer Prize winning poet.

A Safari of African Cooking, by Bill Odarty. ...... cloth 0-910296-72-3 $5.95, paper 0-910296-63-4 3.95

Saint Nigger, by C. E. Cannon. 0-910296-45-6 .... paper 1.00

Song for Nia, by Doughtry Long. 0-910296-64-2 .... paper 1.50

Spirits Unchained, by Keorapetse Kgositsile. 910296-01-4 .... tape $5.00, book 1.00

Sugarfields, by Barbara Mahone. (Distributed by Broadside Press) 1.25

The Rocks Cry Out, by Beatrice M. Murphy and Nancy L. Arnez. 910296-16-2 ... tape $5.00, book 1.00

The Treehouse and Other Poems, by James A. Emanuel. 910296-17-0 .... tape $5.00, book 1.00
  Terse lyrics by widely published young poet.

Think Black, by Don L. Lee. 910296-03-0 .... 1.00

We a BaddDDD People, by Sonia Sanchez. 910296-27-8 .... tape $5.00, paper 1.50

We the Black Woman, by Femi Funmi Ifetayo. (Black Arts Publications) 1.00

We Walk the Way of the New World, by Don L. Lee. 910296-26-X .. tape $5.00, cloth $4.50, paper 1.50
  Don Lee's fourth book is "softer, but louder."

The Youth Makes the Revolution, by Sonebeyatta Amungo (Black Arts Publications) 1.00